Timeless Wealth Management

by Tom Warburton

Timeless Wealth Management
ISBN: 978-1-942451-00-6
Copyright © 2014 by Tom Warburton

Published by
Yorkshire Publishing
6271 East 120th Court
Suite 200
Tulsa, Oklahoma 74137

Text Design: Lisa Simpson
www.SimpsonProductions.net

ACKNOWLEDGMENTS

The author would like to thank Roger Bey, Ph.D.; David Booth; Dave Butler, CFA; Jim Davis, Ph.D.; Bob Deere; Jake DeKinder, CFA; Nobel Laureate Eugene F. Fama; Kenneth R. French, Ph.D.; Mark Gochnour, CFA/CPA; Dr. Steve Greene; Mark Hebner; Marlena Lee, Ph.D.; Bryan McClune, CFA; Dr. Mary Ann Norfleet; Aaron Olson; Gerard O'Reilly, Ph.D.; Jim Parker; Dave Plecha, CFA; Michael Preis, CFA; and Weston Wellington for generously sharing their time, patiently enduring my many questions, indulging in the occasional debate, and inspiring me with their research.

DEDICATION

This book is dedicated to Clyde Stephens and Debbie Viets for teaching me how to live well—and the importance of living well always.

TABLE OF CONTENTS

FOREWORD

Every day my email inbox is full of advice, suggestions, and forecasts as to what dividend stocks to buy; what is going to be the next breakthrough technology; what stocks to short; why emerging markets are going to soar; why emerging markets are going to fall; why gold should be purchased as a hedge; why gold isn't a good investment; why the housing market is going to bust; why the housing market is going to boom; why the Dow Jones is going to 50,000; and why the Dow Jones is going to 10,000. The recommendations, all written with great conviction, go on and on. This plethora of recommendations reminds me of the children's books *Where's Waldo?* Somewhere in all of these emails, there probably is someone for some time period who is correct. Unfortunately, I have no way to identify either who is correct or for what time period the advice applies.

In contrast to the stock picking and market timing strategies that dominate the foregoing recommendations, Tom Warburton's wealth-building strategy follows the best economic theories, which have been subjected to rigorous empirical testing. His diversification and asset allocation strategy does not provide great cocktail party talk. Clients can't brag about the stock that went up ten times, (a ten bagger), but clients also do not have to talk about the great tax write-offs they had on the stocks that went bankrupt.

In *Timeless Wealth Management*, Tom reveals the advice and financial strategies he has provided to his clients for the past eight years. The consistency of his advice, although not unique, is unusual for the investment advising world. Investors should compare the consistency of their financial advisor's advice against the principles outlined in *Timeless Wealth Management*. Then they should determine if they are on the optimal course for wealth independence or whether adjustments in their portfolios and financial strategies are required.

Tom's presentation of some of the leading financial theories that have resulted in Nobel Prizes in Economics, and are the basis for Modern Portfolio Theory, is done in an entertaining manner. He does not present new theories or forecasts. His goal is to provide in an interesting and useful manner the fundamental financial principles that will allow investors to make work optional.

Roger P. Bey
Professor Emeritus of Finance
University of Tulsa

A Personal Note from the Author

Several years ago one of my clients was visiting our office and asked, "So, Tom, tell me what you believe today that's different than what you believed the last time we met." Without hesitation, I responded, "If I ever tell you that I don't believe today what I believed in the past, you should withdraw your money from our stewardship and find a new advisor."

The foregoing is not to imply that I'm not learning all of the time, because I am. My life is an endless stream of visiting with informed and uninformed market participants, digesting academic white papers, and reading wealth management journals.

My point is that the unbiased, peer-reviewed, academic evidence that constituted and constitutes the foundation of my advice has been proven to be accurate—and it is timeless.

This book compiles a series of letters and emails that I've written over many years, which have included massive bull and bear market cycles. Having revisited these missives of yesteryear, I firmly believe that the financial science elaborated then remains as valid today as it was when it was originally composed.

I have three purposes in sharing the compilation of these missives:

1) I am on a crusade to educate investors.

2) I am on a crusade to expose traditional wealth management—stock picking and market timing—as fruitless.

3) I am on a crusade to help investors make work optional and achieve their goals.

Investing is a statistical exercise. Although traditional money managers may want you to believe it's different this time, academic evidence reveals that, when it comes to expectations for long-term or short-term investments in stocks and bonds, trends (and the absence of trends) emerge that are as obvious as 2+2=4.

Knowledge is an investor's friend in the quest for wealth accumulation that is sufficient to make work optional.

Knowledge aids in the challenge of overcoming emotions and enabling practical, proper, and often difficult financial decision-making.

Knowledge is the most powerful tool in the toolbox when it comes to winning the battle to maintain all-important discipline.

The uniquely personal balance between practical decisions and emotional stress lead to goal conflict in a bear market. Emotional response to a bear market frequently leads to bad decision-making. Informed investors will utilize peer-reviewed academic research as the cornerstone for their decision-making process, formulate a well-reasoned plan and then get along with their lives while the markets do what the markets do.

Trusting that you will find this compilation to be entertaining, interesting and, hopefully, useful, I remain:

Yours truly,
Tom Warburton

CHAPTER 1

Pre-Obama . . . But Would It Have Mattered?

The financial markets generally are unpredictable. So that one has to have different scenarios. . . . The idea that you can actually predict what's going to happen contradicts my way of looking at the market. —George Soros

Concentrated Positions

Which stock should you buy now? Jim Cramer says one thing; *Money Magazine* says something else. There are so many contradictory "hot tips" flying around that it is overwhelming and confusing.

A Perspective to Consider

From Harry M. Markowitz, Nobel Prize Winning Economist best known for his pioneering work in "Modern Portfolio

Theory" studying the effects of asset risk, correlation, and diversification on expected investment portfolio returns:

> *"Concentrated investments add risk with no additional expected return. Diversification reduces uncertainty."*

Our Translation

Do not buy any individual stocks ever! (We call this the "Markowitz Rule.")

We spend all day every day talking with people about their money, their investments, and their ability to "sustain their lifestyle." We see horrible things happen to portfolios when investors naively or willingly violate the Markowitz Rule.

Example: SemGroup. We observed a sad example of the damage possible to your net worth with a concentrated investment. SemGroup Energy Partners LP (SGLP) went public with great promise at about $30 per share, bounced around in the $20s subsequent to its initial public offering (IPO) and then dramatically plunged over 50% on one trading day followed by another 25% on the next trading day.

Massive drops in price per share can happen to any individual stock.

It's not just individual stocks that collapse. A collapse can happen to an entire sector. Look no further than the financial sector (Citigroup, Bank of America, JPMorgan Chase,

Wachovia, and others) to observe the imprudence of a concentrated sector position.

It's not unusual for an individual stock or a sector to decline dramatically.

It is unusual for all equity markets to decline simultaneously.

We've observed only five quarters in the last 20 years (80 Quarters ended 12/31/2010) where the U.S. large cap, U.S. small cap, EAFE, BRIC, and REIT markets all simultaneously declined.

Our Advice

Learn about the capital markets. Identify an earnest steward to help you with your stocks and bonds. Develop realistic expectations about returns and volatility. Ignore "hot tips" and "get rich quick" schemes.

Negative Outlook

We've all heard negative outlooks on our economy. "If Obama gets elected then our economy will be crippled by taxes to fund social programs." "If McCain gets elected then our economy will be crippled by taxes to fund the war." "The dollar is rapidly losing value against foreign currencies." The alarmist comments go on-and-on.

A Perspective to Consider

From Warren Buffett—*Fortune Magazine*, "What Warren Thinks" April 14, 2008:

> *"Even if you knew what was going to happen in the economy, which you probably don't, you still wouldn't know what was going to happen in the stock market."*

Our Translation

Investors should not think that what they read in today's paper is important for their investment strategy. Economies go through cycles of recovery, peak, slowdown, and recession. Similarly, stock markets also have cycles. Evidence demonstrates that a strong correlation between "the economy" and "the market" does not exist. There have been many periods in the U.S. economy in the last century wherein there has been a very weak link between the performance of our economy and the stock market.

The wild card in stock market valuations is investor sentiment. For instance, the lowering of interest rates typically has a lagging impact on the economy, but it may impact stock markets immediately, showing a weak correlation between the economy and the stock market.

Likewise, investors have to bear in mind that in a bear market, even if GDP grows, the stock market may not reward the performance. Again, this shows a weak correlation between the economy and the stock market.

Neither our economy nor our stock markets are going to do well every day, every week, or even every year. Excesses must be absorbed. Reasonable expectations demand that we expect economic cycles and stock market cycles.

While we believe that fundamental economic growth dictates stock market advances over the long term, there are short-term setbacks to be endured. This is one of the key reasons that investors need a long-term strategy before investing in stocks. Patience is an important virtue to bring to the game, as far as serious investors are concerned.

Our Advice

The sooner you learn to concern yourself with long-term results, ignore the information spewing out of televisions, and leaping off the front pages of newspapers/magazines, the sooner you are on your way to success as an investor.

WHEN I SAY YOU CAN'T

One time, a youngster was in my office. He was a well-educated and very bright young man who was somewhat intoxicated with self-confidence. He proffered that he could make over 30% annually trading stocks without regard to whether the markets were moving up or down.

A Perspective to Consider

From Ken French, Ph.D., Professor of Finance at the Tuck School of Business at Dartmouth College, well-known within the investment community for his research of the size/value effect and co-author (with Eugene Fama) of the Three-Factor Model (*CFA Magazine,* Sept.-Oct. 2005):

"When I Say 'You Can't Beat The Market,' I Mean You!"

Our Translation

If you think you or anybody else can consistently beat the market through clever stock picking, market timing, sector rotation, or any other means, you are naïve and probably on the road to long-term market underperformance.

Further, if you think you or anybody else can consistently identify market-beating mutual funds or stock pickers in advance, you face odds worse than a tourist in Las Vegas.

The vast majority of would-be market-beating mutual funds underperform their corresponding S&P Index over five-year periods. Over longer periods, the percentage of would-be market-beaters shrinks consistently to low single digits. Nobody wins every single year. (Data courtesy of Standard and Poor's Indices Versus Active Funds Scorecard)

Individual investors attempting to beat the market averaged 3.70% per year for the 20-year period ending December

31, 2004. During this same period, the S&P 500 advanced at a 13.20% annually compounded rate (Dalbar Research).

Hedge funds—the guys that practically guaranteed absolute returns—can't even keep their doors open. Hedge fund closures are occurring at an accelerating rate, and the number of new funds started is off nearly 50% from 2007 (*Wall Street Journal*, June 17, 2008, "Shakeout Roils Hedge Fund World").

Bill Miller, the legendary manager of the Legg Mason Fund who succeeded in beating the market for 15 straight years, finally ran out of luck. He went down 29% in one year and ranked in the bottom 1% of his peer group of fund managers.

In summary: An analysis of unbiased data leads any thoughtful person to conclude you can't beat the market and simply capturing the market will grow your wealth at a very handsome rate (patience is required).

Our Advice

It is important for each of us to acquire realistic expectations about what we can and cannot achieve in the stock market. The stock market provides us with relative returns, not absolute returns. There have been twelve-month periods when we have observed returns in excess of 60% and inferior to −30% from stock portfolios. Most years, expect something in the middle. (The preceding defines "realistic expectations.")

Forget about attempting to generate 30% returns year after year. I've never seen it done and do not believe it to be possible.

All available data suggests that Market Rates Of Return are what good looks like. Don't get down in the dumps when market volatility rains on your inter-period parade, and don't get too giddy when the market makes you look like a genius!

SHOULD I TIME THE MARKET?

Once my buddy Ed said to me back in early 2008, "I played golf with the very smart manager of a local stock brokerage house, and he told me that if Obama gets elected the stock market is going to collapse and we should put all of our money in municipal bonds." A little shocked, I thought, *That sounds like market timing based on a presidential election.*

A Perspective to Consider

From John C. Bogle, founder of the Vanguard Group and widely viewed as one of the investment industry's four "Giants of the Twentieth Century" (*Common Sense on Mutual Funds— New Imperatives for the Intelligent Investor*):

> "*The idea that a bell rings to signal when investors should get into or out of the stock market is simply not credible. After nearly fifty years in this business, I do not know of anybody who has done it successfully and consistently. I*

*don't even know anybody who knows anybody who has
done it successfully and consistently."*

Our Translation

Current events, alarmist headlines, and even a weak economy are not predictive of future stock market performance.

A brief analysis of market commentary and forecasts over the past several decades yields the following.

1973: "The only way that the United States can scrape through the next several years without major economic and social disruptions is to ease off dramatically on energy consumption" (*TIME* ,"The Arabs' New Oil Squeeze: Dimouts, Slowdowns, Chills," November 19, 1973).

- 5 years later the S&P 500 had lost 6.2%.

- 10 years later the S&P 500 had gained 63.9%.

1978: "Financial markets at home and abroad have been devastated in recent weeks as frantic traders and investors scrambled to come to grips with the anti-inflation policies of the Carter Administration and the Federal Reserve Board. After a nervous September, Wall Street succumbed to despair, and the stock market was bloodied by what is being called the October massacre"(John M. Lee, "Tumult in the Markets," *New York Times,* November 6, 1978).

- 5 years later the S&P 500 had gained 70.6%.

- 10 years later the S&P 500 had gained 190.3%.

1989:"The next recession won't look like any that has preceded it in recent decades. We are so heavily indebted that a slump would quickly turn into a Latin American-style depression"(Ashby Bladen, "Borrowing to the Bitter End," *Forbes,* September 4, 1989).

- 5 years later the S&P 500 had gained 33.1%.

- 10 years later the S&P 500 had gained 283.7%.

1991:"Falling real estate prices and the fragile state of the banking system make this recession unlike any other and extremely difficult to forecast" (John R. Dorfman, "First Boston's Bear, Carmine Grigoli, Refuses to Stop Growling Despite Stocks' Big Rally," *Wall Street Journal,* February 7, 1991. Quotation attributed to Carmine Grigoli, Chief Investment Strategist, First Boston Corp.).

- 5 years later the S&P 500 had gained 82.3%.

- 10 years later the S&P 500 had gained 276.1%.

1994: "We're going into one of those long periods where the market does nothing except consolidate this huge move up we've had Dow 4000 is going to be with us for a long time"(Daniel Kadlec, "Will Weary Legs End 20-Year Bull Ride?"*USA TODAY,* December 6, 1994. Quotation attributed to Seth Glickenhaus, Senior Partner, Glickenhaus & Co.).

- 5 years later the S&P 500 had gained 214.1%.

- 10 years later the S&P 500 had gained 162.7%.

In summary, stock markets advance over the long haul because the collective earnings of the stocks that define the markets increase. Stock markets fluctuate up and down day to day due to emotional reactions to news that is not correlated to whether companies grow over the long haul.

Our Advice

Acquire emotional neutrality. Forget about managing your portfolio based on alarmist headlines or the state of the economy. Manage your portfolio based on your personal financial situation. Change your portfolio if your personal financial situation changes.

Acquire knowledge about the capital markets. Be purposeful about your allocation to stocks and bonds. Understand that stocks are more volatile than bonds, and the reward for withstanding that volatility is probably significantly greater wealth accumulation and goal achievement. Understand that bonds deliver steadier appreciation than stocks, and the punishment for that consistency is a rate of return that is likely to do little more than slightly out-pace inflation and out-perform cash. Understand that your allocation to stocks and to bonds in your portfolio will predict the performance (return and volatility) of your portfolio with far greater accuracy than headlines or current economic conditions.

INFLATION RISK

I talked with a good friend who is in his late sixties. Appearing confident, he leaned back in his big leather chair and said, "I don't see why I need to take any stock market risk. I've got plenty of money. I'm going to invest it all in bonds and relax." A little surprised, I wondered for a moment if my buddy had forgotten about the high inflation rates of the '70s.

A Perspective to Consider

From Louis Pasteur, French chemist and microbiologist best known for inventing "pasteurization," a method to stop milk and wine from causing sickness.

"Chance favors the prepared mind."

Our Translation

"Chance favors the prepared portfolio." The chance of outliving your money is much higher if you prepare improperly and invest too conservatively in retirement.

I know a number of folks who retired in their sixties with, what appeared to be, an ample amount of money. They invested their money entirely in bonds. Over the decades, the required cash flow for lifestyle drawn from their portfolios combined with the modest interest from their bond portfolios reduced their purchasing power to the point that their standard of living required substantial compromise.

Many investors ask the question: "How much income can I safely take from my portfolio for general living expenses?" That's the wrong question. The more accurate question is: "How much can I safely spend from my portfolio for general living expenses?"

Income and cash flow are not the same thing. "Income" is the amount of dividend and interest earned by a portfolio that, in the case of a taxable account, you would pay income taxes on. "Cash flow" is the amount of money you need for living expenses.

It's misguided for the majority of investors to think in terms of deriving necessary cash flow solely from portfolio income without invading principal. This is a detrimental emotional bias.

In summary: Your focus should be on total after-tax return (dividends plus interest plus capital gains). Selling stock for cash flow can be a better alternative than generating taxable income due to the simple arbitrage between ordinary-income tax rates and long-term capital-gains rates.

Our Advice

Prepare your mind for the likelihood of inflation and reality of taxes.

Many of us are going to live well into our nineties. In 30 years, it may take more than $10 to purchase what $1 will purchase today. A very comfortable nest egg of $2,000,000 today could become a very uncomfortable amount (in terms of purchasing power) in only a few decades, which will fly by very quickly.

Many investors define the word "risk" as "the possibility of losing your money." I suggest that the risk of losing your purchasing power to inflation should not be ignored.

The appropriate allocation of your portfolio to stocks and bonds is the most important decision you can make to preserve your purchasing power.

Chapter 1 Summary

- Diversification reduces uncertainty.

- It's not unusual for an individual stock or a sector to decline dramatically

- The 'Wild Card' in stock market valuations is "investor sentiment."

- When I Say 'You Can't Beat The Market' I Mean You!

- Chance favors the prepared portfolio

CHAPTER 2

THE BEST TIME TO INVEST IS . . .

Time flies over us, but leaves its shadow behind. —
Nathaniel Hawthorne

I had a buddy with a great business, a lot of money, a modest lifestyle, and who had already salted away a significant nest egg. He had accumulated a considerable amount of cash in his checking account and was trying to figure out whether or not to invest it now or wait until the market "turns around."

A Perspective to Consider

From Sir John Templeton, legendary investor, billionaire, and mutual fund pioneer who dedicated much of his fortune to religion and science.

"The best time to invest is when you have money. This is because history suggests it is not timing the markets that matters; it is time in the market."

Our Translation

"If you have surplus cash you should invest it now."

The miracle of compound interest is, as Albert Einstein said, "the most powerful force in the universe." It won't benefit you if you sit on the sidelines.

From December 31, 1926,through December 31, 2007 (81 years), the following annually compounded rates of return were produced:

- 10.4%,S&P 500 Index

- 11.2%, U.S. Large Cap Value Fama/French Index

- 9.4%, U.S. Large Cap Growth Fama/French Index

- 14.0%, U.S. Small Cap Value Fama/French index

- 12.2%, U.S. Small Cap Fama/French Index

- 9.3%, U.S. Small Cap Growth Fama/French Index

Let's not forget that these RORs were achieved in all kinds of turmoil—the Great Depression, World War II, the Cuban Missile Crisis, the stagflation era, interest rate cycles, real estate debacles, and the Internet bubble, to name a few.

Question: What do these numbers really represent? Answer: The fruits of democracy, free enterprise, and capitalism!

Many investors ask the question: "Which direction is the stock market going this year"?

Nobody knows the answer to that question. The important question is: "How long can I wait for the stock market to go up"?

In summary: The stock market has historically provided very attractive returns over the long haul. If you had the patience, courage and staying power to ride out bear markets you were consistently rewarded with bull markets.

Democracy, free enterprise, and capitalism drive enterprise appreciation and are at the heart of long-term market advances.

Our Advice

If you have surplus cash that you don't need for lifestyle or debt service, you should invest it now and wait patiently for "the fruits of democracy, free enterprise and capitalism" to grow your wealth.

View market declines as an opportunity to buy bargains.

Understand that short-term market fluctuations are inevitable. Don't get depressed over a down move or exhilarated by an up move.

Market declines and advances are simply different folds in the same fabric.

Markets Fluctuate

Our primary objective is for our clients to achieve their goals. Clearly, we enjoy market advances as it makes our clients wealthier and everybody feels better when they have more money. We are disappointed when there is a lack of appreciation of our clients' portfolios. Although we can't take credit for stock market advances or responsibility for stock market declines, we do sympathize with frustrated investors.

While we lament a flat stock market, it is healthy to remember things could always be much worse. Since 1926, there have been several instances of the S&P 500 declining by more than 40% over two-year periods.

Frankly, I expect that over the coming decades we will experience dramatic market declines to test our resolve and dramatic Market advances to make us giddy. Risk and return are inextricably related. Volatility and returns have been observed throughout history.

The Boston Snow Indicator

Once a buddy called and said, "We didn't have a white Christmas last winter in Boston!" Intrigued, I judiciously responded, "What?" He smugly advised, "Well Tom, the Boston Snow Indicator states that a white Christmas in Boston will result in rising stock prices for the following year!"

A Perspective to Consider

From Edgar R. Fiedler, widely respected professional economist from his 1977 classic *The Three Rs of Economic Forecasting—Irrational, Irrelevant and Irreverent*

"He who lives by the crystal ball soon learns to eat ground glass."

Our Translation

As you may have guessed, there is no logical correlation between whether there is snow in Boston on Christmas and the performance of the stock market. Any incidence of a white Christmas in Boston and bullish market performance in the following year are purely coincidental. (This may be why the Boston Snow Indicator is also referred to as the "B.S. Indicator.")

A thorough analysis of would-be market indicators leads one to conclude there are dozens of BS Indicators.

Based on entertainment value, my favorite indicators are:

- The Hemline Indicator—If you want to know which way the stock market is headed, watch the direction of women's dresses."Bull Markets, Bare Knees."

- The Bikini Indicator—When an American graced the cover of the *Sports Illustrated* "Swimsuit Issue," the S&P 500 gained an average of 13.9%.

- Based on useful information my favorite indicator is The Equity Indicator—Equities outperform bonds over statistically significant periods of time.

Stock ownership conveys equity rights to a company that entitles the shareholder to share in the earnings that may occur and accrue. Some of these earnings may be paid out as dividends while the rest are retained. The retained earnings are used to build infrastructure, giving the company the ability to generate even greater future earnings. As the earnings continue to rise, the price of the stock will normally rise as well.

If you apply this observation to individual stocks, you may be in for a rude awakening. Bizarre things happen to individual companies. If you apply this observation to the global stock market, a very attractive outcome becomes more likely.

Throughout recorded history, the aggregate value of global stock markets has grown significantly over time. I expect this aggregate value to continue to grow.

I like the Equity Indicator. I like having equity rights to the global stock market by owning an equity stake in almost 14,000 companies currently traded in over 40 different countries that offer suitably regulated public equity markets.

Do I expect the value of the global stock markets to grow each and every year? Heck no! I expect negative returns one year out of every three, and sometimes two years in a row. I also expect bonds to outperform stocks one year out of every three, and sometimes three years in a row.

Whereas there is no tool or indicator that enables us to consistently predict positive or negative years in advance, I am content to wait patiently while the irrationalities of stock market exuberance and stock market draw-downs work themselves out.

Our Advice

- Do not be seduced by Boston Snowstorms and do not eat any ground glass.

- Do not waste your time trying to figure out which money center bank is the best investment or whether the stock market is due for a correction.

- Become, and view yourself as, an equity holder in global capitalism happy to ride out anything that Wall Street mavens throw at you in anticipation of long-term growth of wealth.

CHAPTER 3

Big Bear

In 2008, people who invested in hedge funds needed capital badly, but many of the funds would not return their money. However, I gave money back to any investor who requested it. It was the bottom of the market and a pretty tough time. —Carl Icahn

Where Do Hedge Funds Enrich

A few years back, I spoke with a buddy in New York City who works for a globally prominent wealth management firm serving the ultra-high net worth crowd. He was giddy about how his clients were buying hedge funds. He was making a bundle. He never commented on how his clients were doing. Let's look at the illusionary benefits and real risks of hedge funds.

A Perspective to Consider

From Burton G. Malkiel, Princeton University Professor of Economics and author of *A Random Walk Down Wall Street*, and managing principal of Atanu Saha Analysis Group, New York City, as quoted in the *Financial Analysts Journal*, November/December 2005:

"We conclude that hedge funds are far riskier and provide much lower returns than is commonly supposed."

Our Translation

Hedge funds are little more than fancy mutual funds with:

- Little or no transparency,

- Little or no regulatory oversight,

- Exorbitant fees,

- Outrageous bonuses paid to managers for short-term luck,

- Reckless leverage,

- Sexy advertisements to lure investors, and

- Long-Term annualized compound rates of return, in aggregate, inferior to that of a well-reasoned globally diversified portfolio of stocks.

Alfred Winslow Jones formed the first hedge fund in 1949. Mr. Jones genuinely "hedged" his long positions by short-selling similar positions. With this approach, Mr. Jones generated returns inferior to stocks with less volatility than a long only portfolio.

Today, the word "hedge' is often a misnomer in understanding what hedge funds do. Whereas a hedge fund is defined as "any private pool of capital organized for investment purposes," Pandora's box has been opened for an environment of excess. Genuine hedging has given way to rampant speculation fueled by excessive leverage.

Witness the collapse of Amaranth Capital that lost $5 billion in a week—this from a hedge fund that boasted world-class risk-management.

Witness the collapse of the Bear Stearns High Grade fund that had been profitable every month since inception prior to the weight of leverage-fueled wrong-way bets on mortgage-backed securities.

"They borrowed money to double-down on losing positions" is a phrase you will read repeatedly if you search the web to research hedge fund failures.

Enough of the anecdotes, here are the five basic reasons I hate hedge funds:

The Risks: "The risks facing hedge funds are non-linear and more complex than those facing traditional asset classes . . . such risks are currently not widely appreciated or well-understood."—Andrew Lo, MIT.

The Returns: "We conclude that hedge funds are far riskier and provide much lower returns than is commonly supposed."—Malkiel and Saha, "Hedge Funds: Risk and Return," Financial Analysts Journal; Nov/Dec 2005.

The Expenses: "Our research has shown that in at least 80% of cases the after-fee alpha for hedge funds is negative. . . . I'm not saying they don't have skill; I'm just saying they don't have enough skill to make up for their fees."—John Cassidy, "Hedge Clipping," *New Yorker*, July 2, 2007.

The Myth: "The term 'absolute-return investing' has no meaning. It misleads the listener into thinking it has substance that it does not have, and in our opinion, the term simply should not be used."—M. Barton Waring and Laurence B. Siegel, "The Myth of the Absolute-Return Investor," *Financial Analysts Journal*, March/April 2006.

Fund of Funds: All of the problems with ordinary hedge funds cited above are applicable to the fund of funds. The article by Malkiel and Saha cited above shows that the fund of funds category achieved a return that was 5.7% lower than the S&P 500. (The entire hedge fund universe was 3.5% lower than the SP 500.)

Being wealthy or smart does not entitle anybody to beat the market or cheat risk, nor does it imbue them with clairvoyance.

If you are interested in Warren Buffett's view on this subject, visit "Buffett's Big Bet" from *Fortune* magazine, June 9, 2008 (in archive).

Our Advice

Do not be seduced by the allure of that which can't be delivered. Returns that sound too good to be true are just that—too good to be true.

Do not think that just because somebody is really smart or charges a really high fee they will be able to pick the best grains of sand off the beach.

There are over 23,000 stocks for sale in the global equity markets. Collectively these stocks have appreciated or declined at unpredictable rates over short periods of time and appreciated at attractive rates over long periods of time. There is no evidence of any clever stock picker, market timer, mutual fund manager, or hedge fund outperforming the market over a statistically significant period of time.

In our view, hedge funds will one day be viewed as "financial hula hoops." I hope my buddy, who was giddy about how much money he was making by selling them to his clients, developed a conscience and reflected, "Where were my ethics?"

As I walked into my office building in the midst of a bear market, the people I saw in the lobby, the attorneys on the elevator, and even the last bastions of risk-tolerant professionals (the oil and gas guys) asked me "So, are you going upstairs to sell all your stocks?"

In contrast, I was feeling good that my monthly auto-deposit hit Monday morning and I had been a buyer at the close of that week's Monday 500-point Dow decline. Selling was the farthest thing from my mind!

A Perspective to Consider

From Warren Buffett, the Oracle of Omaha:

> *"Stocks are the only thing that
> people won't buy when they are on sale."*

Our Translation

It's natural to be nervous when all the news is negative. Televisions are glowing with red numbers. Newspapers publish bad news in giant-sized bold print. Radio commentators predict the end of the world as we know it.

Okay, so the Fannie/Freddie bailout is now on the books, rivals purchased Merrill Lynch and Bear Stearns while Lehman Brothers' headed into bankruptcy. Was there more bad news yet to come? You bet.

Did this imply that free market capitalism was over? No. The stage was set for fortunes to be made and enhanced.

Alan Greenspan was levelheaded on Bloomberg TV when he said, "Investors overlook the fact that whenever there is a loser there is a winner." The clients from the failed firms had to go somewhere. Being from Kansas, I summed this up simply:"There has to be a pony in here somewhere!"

It's unfortunate that the performance-based compensation practices on Wall Street were structured to pay big bonuses when bankers bet right, but imposed losses only on share-holders when the bankers bet wrong. This mentality led to the failure of the auction-rate securities market and the mortgage-backed securities meltdown, and may yet lead to another round of bank failures if counter-party failure leads to a collapse of the derivatives/swap spider-web.

I find it interesting that the size and status of the big, old, and venerable firms permitted them to dig a hole too deep for sunlight.

It's likewise interesting that investors went to these same big, old, and venerable firms seeking objective investment advice. What investors too often received was conflicted advice delivered by advisers generating commissions by selling fancy, complex, and wacky products guaranteed by "the full faith and credit" of the selling firm with unintelligible risks obscurely disclosed in fine print.

For the record, independent registered investment advisors (RIAs) are different from the venerable firms. RIAs are legally required to provide objectivity, and do not accept compensation from anyone but their clients in the form of transparent fees. Additionally, RIAs are required to take on a fiduciary duty to their clients and receive no incentive for using in-house products. Most RIAs don't have any in-house products. The job of an RIA is to find the best possible strategy for an investor at a fair and reasonable price, acting again, in a fiduciary manner. This is not the case at brokerage houses or Wall Street firms with an ever-growing number of new products to sell.

Unfortunately, taxpayers will absorb some of the restructuring costs of these troubled institutions. Thousands of brokers will jump ship to perform their mischief elsewhere. Millions of investors won't know to whom to turn for their next fleecing. Meanwhile, trillions of dollars are stranded with no shortage of unanswered questions.

Obviously, all investors owning shares in Bear Stearns, Lehman, or Merrill were affected to some degree. Mutual funds with concentrated positions in these firms experienced significant draw-downs.

However, well diversified global portfolios were minimally affected by the failure of that handful of firms. We avoided concentrated positions by owning almost 14,000 in stocks in over 40 different countries.

Our Advice

Do you have a financial advisor? Why do the wealthiest families and large endowments engage financial advisors? A financial advisor is similar to a coach. Tiger Woods at one point was, arguably, the world's greatest athlete, yet he appreciated the value of a coach. Wealthy families and large endowments are like Tiger Woods. They appreciate the value of specialized expertise and objective advice.

If you have a financial advisor and a sound plan, you should probably do nothing more than have a chat.

If you don't have a financial advisor, you should find one. See if your portfolio and your plan make sense. Determine if there are indistinct risks or contingent liabilities that need to be provided for. Don't procrastinate—do it now!

For the record, I enjoyed walking into my building the next morning and asking my buddies, "How many dollars did you invest in the stock market Tuesday?"

HOW SAFE ARE MY INVESTMENTS?

One week, I took my mom out on our weekly car ride to Braum's for ice cream, down Riverside Drive for fun and to Walmart for necessities. During the course of our drive, Mom asked, "How safe are my investments?"

A Perspective to Consider

From William Penn Adair "Will" Rogers, Oklahoma's Favorite Son, Cherokee-American cowboy, comedian, humorist, social commentator, vaudeville performer, and actor in the depths of the Depression:

> *"I'm not concerned about the return on my money. I'm concerned about the return of my money!"*

An Overview of Risks

Investors in the stock and bond markets face three primary risks:

1) Custodian risk—can I get my money back?

2) Systemic risk—what are the risks common to an entire market?

3) Non-systemic risk—what are the risks of owning individual securities?

Custodian Risk: You give your money to a person or a firm. When you call them up and tell them you want it back, do they have the financial wherewithal to return it? Example: Deposits in a failed bank in excess of the FDIC $100,000 insurance. Maybe you will collect and maybe you won't.

Systemic Risk: The value of the stock market fluctuates more dramatically than the value of the bond market. Example: An investment in the S&P 500 has increased at 10.4% annually compounded since 1925 and has produced negative returns 23 out of 83 years. An investment in U.S. one-month treasuries has increased at 3.7% annually compounded since 1925 and has produced positive returns every year. The chances of the entire stock or bond market going to zero are very low.

Non-Systemic Risk: Individual securities sometimes lose value with little hope of a future increase. Examples would be Enron, WorldCom, and Lehman Brothers. The chance of any individual stock going to zero is a genuine risk that must be considered.

An Overview of Risks for Our Clients

What is the custodian risk for our clients? The custodian of our client portfolios is TD Ameritrade-Institutional (TDAI). (We hold no client funds at Warburton Capital.)TDAI holds client securities and generates revenue by facilitating trades in client accounts. TDAI is a member of the Securities Investor Protection Corporation (SIPC), which protects securities in an account. Additional insurance is provided by London Insurers. SIPC and London Insurers provide protection against broker-age insolvency and do not protect against loss in market value of securities.

What is the systemic risk for our clients? Our stock portfolios hold almost 14,000 stocks from over 40 different countries. Our bond portfolios hold investment grade bonds from over a dozen different countries. What would it take for the value of this broadly diversified portfolio of stocks and bonds to go to zero? A complete collapse of society? We are comfortable investing our client portfolios, and our personal portfolios, in global capitalism believing that—if this fails—there is no safe harbor.

What is the non-systemic risk for our clients? There is almost none. We never concentrate our investments in any single stock, country or sector. To do so would violate the very principles of modern financial science that our methodology is based on. When your investments are diversified across thousands of companies and investment-grade bonds, the collapse of a handful of firms doesn't even dent the fender of your portfolio.

We have identified what we believe to be a trustworthy custodian (TDAI) who offers their services at an attractive price. We are long-only, broadly diversified investors in cash, bonds, stocks and REIT's (Real Estate Investment Trusts). We purposefully allocate to domestic/foreign, large/small, and growth/value in a manner that has worked out attractively for decades. We do not employ leverage. We do not engage in short-selling. We do not offer exotic "structured products" with counter-party obligations that may or may not work out.

The greatest risk to our methodology is the survival of the cash, stock, and bond markets, which, in our view, depends on the survival of free market capitalism. We are not worried about the survival of free market capitalism, and we believe in the resilience of economies and the ingenuity of the human race. History shows us that many great challenges have been overcome.

BEAR MARKET OF SUBSTANTIAL PROPORTIONS

In the past, the market has strained the patience of many investors. As of the market close on Tuesday, October 7, 2008, the S&P 500 was down 36% from its high of 1565.15 on October 9, 2007.

It was a bear market of substantial magnitude.

Of the twelve protracted negative markets since 1949, we have observed only two larger draw-downs. The 1973-74 market was down by 43% before it reversed course. Curiously, the 2000-02 market was also down 43% before the selling abated.

Clearly in late 2008, the market was again "on sale" relative to one year prior. He of the "be fearful when others are greedy and be greedy when others are fearful" mentality, Warren Buffet, made headlines at the time when he put his money where his mouth was by stepping up to buy securities.

What Should an Investor Do?

In our office, we fielded phone calls from clients wanting to know how to react or take advantage of that market. There were four basic options:

1) Make a substantial investment

2) Implement or increase incremental investments

3) Rebalance to a more aggressive strategy

4) Do nothing

Each of these approaches demanded consideration.

Make a substantial investment now: I view this as an aggressive approach. Nobody knew if the market was going to decline further. Putting all of your cash into the market at that time would be viewed as regrettable if we got another 10% decline. Of course, if the market turned around that week, the strategy would be viewed as genius.

Implement or increase incremental investments: I view this as a conservative approach. Most of our clients were enrolled in monthly auto-purchase programs. Some of our clients called to increase the amount of their auto-purchase. If the market went down, our clients would then buy bargains at even deeper discounts. If the market went up, our clients continued to buy at prices well below one year before. I find this approach to be attractive, and it is my personal strategy.

Rebalance to a more aggressive strategy: I hate this idea. Our clients' asset allocations were designed to be "all weather," and the allocations exist for a purpose that has to do with achieving a financial goal. If the asset allocation was proper a year ago, it remains proper today. To rebalance to a more aggressive strategy was a thinly veiled attempt at market timing, and might have resulted in a setback toward goal achievement.

Do nothing: I think this is just fine. It's obvious that markets change, and market change should not dictate a change in behavior. If the financial goal has changed, well, that's a different story.

Custodial Risk

The Fannie/Freddie bailout was on the books. Rivals acquired Merrill Lynch and Bear Stearns. Lehman Brothers collapsed. AIG hoped to pull a rabbit out of a hat. Investors were nervous.

Investors were led to believe that the larger a company is or the longer they have been around, the safer they are. Unfortunately, this is not the case. The size and reputation of the aforementioned firms allowed them the resources to dig very deep holes. It's become clear to me that large banks are exposed to greater risks than smaller banks, and large banks expose their clients to greater risks than smaller banks.

Fueling the financial meltdowns were the performance-based compensation practices at Lehman and throughout Wall Street. Big bonuses were paid to bankers when they bet right, but the shareholders were left holding an empty sack when the bankers bet wrong. This compensation structure, in part, led to the auction-rate securities debacle and the mortgage-backed securities meltdown. Do you really want your banker/advisor to be paid a princely sum for selling you something that you might not need to buy but his or her management team wants him or her to sell?

The most important question for investors is, "Can I get my money back?"

When you deposit your money with a financial institution, one of two things happens:

1) They will place it in an account for you to direct (custodian), or

2) They will turn around and loan/invest it for their benefit (bank).

Custodians simply hold your investments and make their money on trading/holding fees.

Banks, on the other hand, make their money from lending and investing your money. If they invest in poor opportunities, they may fail and you may lose.

The problem for investors is that the distinction between banks and custodians has become increasingly blurred. Most, if not all, of the aforementioned companies were engaged in banking functions, custodial functions, and investment advisory services.

Not surprisingly, the majority of the Wall Street firms directed their employees to sell their proprietary in-house products. Just another revenue center for the Big Boys! Ask yourself, "What are the chances of getting objective advice from an employee of a firm that manufactures securities?" You may go to one of the Big Boy firms for objective investment advice, but most likely, you will not find it.

The result of this marriage between custodians, banks, and securities firms is a conflict of interest. When it played out, many investors were stuck holding in-house investments that were either worth less or worthless.

Let's consider a different business model—the independent Registered Investment Advisor (RIA). RIAs are required to provide objectivity. RIAs offer transparent pricing, do not accept compensation from anyone but their clients, and are not required to sell an investment just because it was cooked up in-house. Further, RIAs are required to take on a fiduciary duty to you, the client.

Warburton Capital is an RIA, and we provide objective advice.

Independent third parties provide our investments. We don't pay them, and they don't pay us. As an independent financial advisory firm, we have no incentive to use in-house products—we don't have any. Our job is to find the best possible strategy for your portfolio at a fair and reasonable price, acting, again, in a fiduciary manner.

The custodian of our client portfolios is TD Ameritrade-Institutional (TDAI).(We hold no client funds at Warburton Capital.) TDAI holds client securities and generates revenue by facilitating trades in client accounts. TDAI is a member of the Securities Investor Protection Corporation (SIPC), which protects securities in an account up to $500.000.Up to an aggregate of $250 million of additional securities protection, of which $900,000 may be applied to cash, is provided by London insurers, also limited to a combined return to any client from a trustee, SIPC and London Insurers of $150 million. This coverage provides protection against brokerage insolvency and does not protect against loss in market value of the securities. *(Dollar amounts may change over time)*.

It's a shame that investors and taxpayers had to absorb the restructuring costs of troubled institutions. It was even more tragic to think how much remained to be decided among the larger firms. There were millions of investors, and trillions of dollars, trapped with a plethora of unanswered questions. Clients of these firms were not sure whom they would be calling a few weeks later, as many brokers from these famed institutions undoubtedly jumped ship. Staying the course is hard enough when you have a sound plan and good advisor, much less without one.

If you owned individual stock in Bear Stearns, Lehman, or Merrill, you were affected. Some active fund managers can own as much as 5% in one individual stock. Therefore, all mutual funds do not necessarily provide the risk-management benefits of diversification. At Warburton Capital, we protect our clients against individual financial risks by having them own the market through enormous diversification. (Our clients own almost 14,000 securities spread out in over 40 different countries.) If you are our client, you enjoy enormous diversification. The bankruptcy of a few firms doesn't even dent the fender of our portfolios. We cannot promise that you will not be affected during a massive market downturn—markets are highly correlated and stocks tend to move in the same direction. But by spreading our investments so broadly, the decline of our portfolios was not as extreme as that of the financial sector, and we are in a nice position to reap rewards swiftly when the broad markets inevitably turn positive.

Although it's not always intuitive, the down times are exactly the times when fortunes are kept and thus bigger fortunes are made in the future. Understanding recent events and questioning outdated Wall Street practices is the first step to wealth management without worry.

At Warburton Capital, we believe in the resilience of free market capitalism and are committed to the long-term success of investor portfolios. If you have any doubts as to whether or not you are properly invested, now is a good time to call us.

CHAPTER 4

EMOTIONS

Horrible year-to-date returns. Volatility beyond recollection. Is this how you feel?

WATCHING THE STOCK MARKET

It really can work on your emotions. What does it do to your mind when you think about it in the headlights of reason?

My buddy Bill was standing in those headlights. He called me and said, "Warburton, I've got it figured out. In 20 years, there are going to be another 1.5 billion people on this planet and they are going to demand goods and services. I believe the goods and services will be provided by free enterprise. I want to increase my monthly auto deposit and benefit down the road!"

Another Perspective to Consider

From Joanna Slater, *Wall Street Journal*, Saturday/Sunday, November 1-2, 2008:

> *"Stocks look cheap world-wide. . . . Valuations are now at a level that appears equivalent to the 1970s."*

What Might It Benefit Investors to Know

First of all, nobody knows when the global equity markets find an inflection point be it either a low point or a high point. No matter how much you think about this, you will never know the answer with any degree of certainty.

Secondly, over the past 60 years, there have been 12 bear markets, lasting an average of 14 months and declining an average of 22.4% before recovering. This current market has significantly exceeded the average to the downside.

Thirdly, the market has always recovered. Over the past 60 years, there have been 12 bull markets, lasting an average of 45 months, each growing an average of 123.9%.

Fourthly, economic recessions have produced bull markets 72% of the time.

So, we stir this into a soup and conclude that:

- There is never any certainty when predicting the stock market.

- Whenever the markets have pulled back 20% there is a high probability that the sell-off will abate.

- The probability is high that the market will recover handsomely.

- Market performance is independent of economic recession.

We don't want to miss opportunities by sitting in cash and trying to figure out if a particular point is the bottom. We do want the high probability odds, and we aren't worried about an economic recession's impact on the stock markets.

Warren Buffett, most of our clients, and we ourselves believe that a downturn is a great time to invest in stocks. Therefore, if the market has declined, it might make sense to increase exposure to stocks.

A Really Great Chart

My buddies at JPMorgan sent me a chart in 2008. This chart revealed the ten-year moving average of returns in U.S. large cap stocks over the trailing 126 years.

It's obvious that the markets move through cycles about every 35 or 40 years.(For the trailing ten years, returns were negligible.)

In between these periods of negligible returns, we observe returns that are genuinely out-sized. (Ten-year annually compounded returns have been in the 15–20% range.)

Does this suggest that in 2008, we were witnessing the buying opportunity of a lifetime?

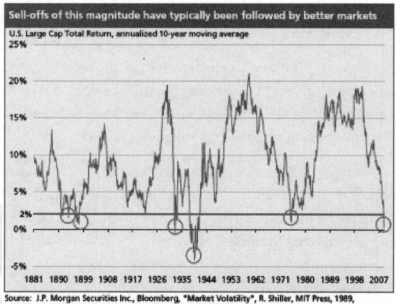

Sell-offs of this magnitude have typically been followed by better markets

U.S. Large Cap Total Return, annualized 10-year moving average

Source: J.P. Morgan Securities Inc., Bloomberg, "Market Volatility", R. Shiller, MIT Press, 1989, and "Irrational Exuberance", Princeton 2005. Data as of October 10, 2008.

"The seeds of out-sized returns are planted in bear markets."—Tom Warburton (thanks to my buddy Terry for inspiration.)

We believe, as do many veteran stock market observers:

- That the 2008 market represented a buying opportunity that only comes along about every 35 or 40 years.

- That we will witness record corporate earnings and global stock markets setting all-time highs over the next 5 to 20 years.

- That fortunes are created by investing when the masses are selling.

Personally, I have committed to my belief by systematically investing via semi-monthly auto-deposit at a rate greater than I was one year ago. If the markets go on down, it will represent little more than an even better buying opportunity.

Discipline

After the worst two months in stock market history in 2008, none of us knew if the market or the economy had hit bottom. Did you find yourself wondering aloud when that would happen? You were not alone.

Although Federal Reserve Chairman Ben Bernanke doesn't look upbeat in the photo, he has gone on record with the following quote:

"Over the years, the U.S. economy has shown a remarkable ability to absorb shocks of all kinds, to recover, and to continue to grow. Flexible and efficient markets for labor

and capital, an entrepreneurial tradition, and a general willingness to tolerate and even embrace technological and economic change all contribute to this resiliency."

Let's just shout it out—we were having a very severe bear market!

Did any of us believe that we would never see another bear market? Bull and bear markets come and go as surely as the seasonal cycles and they are both temporary. Realistic expectations require us to expect economic, stock market, and interest rate cycles.

In full knowledge of market cyclicality and with full faith in Chairman Bernanke's comment, we present our thesis for successful investing:

"Clairvoyance is not needed. Discipline is required."

How Discipline Would Have Worked Out in the Past

Suppose you had invested $100 every month in the S&P 500 index beginning in January 1929. Unfortunately, we didn't have the clairvoyance to know that a market crash and the Great Depression were on the way, so we simply made our $100 monthly investment every single month for the next 30 years in a blindly, disciplined manner.

Here is a chart summarizing how much we would have invested, how much our portfolio would have been worth with all dividends reinvested, and the resultant total gain/(loss) of the portfolio:

Year From Jan 1929	Total Invested	Portfolio Value	Total Gain/(Loss)
1st Year	$ 1,300	$ 1,138	$ (162)
2nd Year	$ 2,500	$ 1,877	$ (623)
3rd Year	$ 3,700	$ 1,967	$ (1,733)
4th Year	$ 4,900	$ 3,186	$ (1,714)
5th Year	$ 6,100	$ 6,176	$ 76
10th Year	$ 12,100	$ 15,859	$ 3,759
20th Year	$ 24,100	$ 44,469	$ 20,369
30th Year	$ 36,100	$ 183,952	$ 147,852

Data source: Professor Robert Shiller's website

Wow! It all worked out pretty well!

Let's not forget that our experiment started just before the worst stock market period in history. Between 1929 and 1934, the stock market produced an 89% decline. An 89% decline! The worst decline in the history of the stock market was a remarkable headwind to overcome.

In our view, the message of this experiment is obvious: To recover from a market crash and to survive a deep recession you don't need clairvoyance. You need discipline, patience, and the resilience of free market capitalism.

Another Perspective: The stock market is volatile. It is today; it has been in the past, and we expect it to be in the future.

In managing our personal portfolios and the portfolios of our clients, we acknowledge the presence of volatility. We eliminate the negative impact of volatility on our financial plans by utilizing our Golden Rule for stock investing:

"Don't invest your gold in the stock market
if you need it in less than fifteen years."

We invest in the stock market with money we don't need for at least fifteen years in anticipation of handsome returns by the end of the fifteen-year period.

We believe that money necessary to finance immediate lifestyle needs should be invested very conservatively in short-term investment-grade global bonds. Over the long haul, these conservative bonds offer attractive principal stability and returns that outpace cash and inflation.

CHAPTER 5

LESSONS FROM 2008

As we all know, the financial markets started poorly in 2008 and got dramatically worse before staging a modest "Santa Claus rally" in late December. What did 2009 have in store? We have no idea at the outset and left such prognostications to the village idiots on CNBC who speculate for the Wall Street firms and make conjecture their stock in trade.

Instead, I watched how the world economy worked itself out of its malaise. My lifelong best friend once told me, "When things are good, it's hard to figure out how they will ever get bad; and when things are bad, it's hard to figure out how they will ever get good."

In light of the overwhelming negative information, it was difficult to figure out how we humans would rebound to a new era of unprecedented prosperity.

Stock Market Performance in 2008

The following chart illustrates the fifteen worst calendar-year performances of the Dow since its inception in 1896:

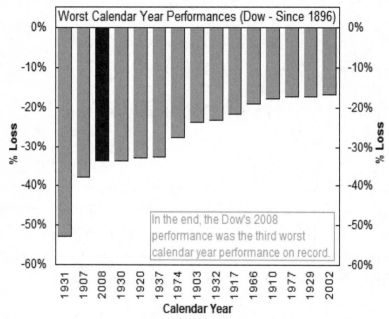

Only 1931 and 1907 produced greater declines than 2008. It is worth noting that major banking crises occurred in 1931, 1907, 2008 and 1930—the four worst calendar years on record in terms of stock market performance.

In a year when many investors' stock portfolios were down by 50% or more, we were pleased to see the decline of our 100% stock portfolio limited to 40.7%. The relative under-performance of our 100% stock portfolio to the S&P 500 is attributable to our 30% allocation to non-U.S. stocks, which we anticipate to be accretive to our returns in the future.

How Do We Expect the Stock and Bond Markets to Perform in the Future?

Since 1926, stocks (the S&P 500) have provided better returns than bonds (one-month Treasury bills) as follows:

- 69% of the time over any 12-month period

- 76% of the time over any 3-year period

- 77% of the time over any 5-year period

- 86% of the time over any 10-year period

- 94% of the time over any 15-year period

- 100% of the time over any 20-year period

Clearly, the house odds are in favor of stocks year after year, and become even more favorable over longer periods.

However, that's not a complete answer. So, permit me to answer the question by first posing a question for each of us market observers. Can you predict whether stocks or bonds will provide superior returns in each of the next ten years and over the next ten-year period?

Do you have a view for 2015 but not beyond? Do you have a view for 10 years from now?

In my view, the year-to-year projections are a crapshoot. It's fun to guess about what will happen each year, but none of us can know with any degree of certainty. Predicting results 10 years out is a safer bet. The likelihood of stocks outperforming bonds over the long haul is so high that it must be viewed as probable. With the probable long-term outperformance of stocks, we incur the likelihood of some great years, some bad years, and the returns being distributed over a wide range. Bonds, on the other hand, generally reward investors with modest but consistent returns.

The question I posed on the previous page and my foregoing discussion are provided to make a point. In our view, the only reasonable investment in the stock market is a long-term investment. 2008 served up a conclusive demonstration that substantial declines are possible just as 2003 demonstrated disproportionate advances are possible. We encourage investors to make reasonable investments in well-reasoned proportions.

We believe the most important decision any investor can make is asset allocation. A good example of this is provided by comments from Dr. Harry Markowitz. Dr. Markowitz shared the Nobel Prize in Economics in 1990 for his mathematical explorations of the relationship between risk and return. Dr. Markowitz was asked how he divided his assets between stocks and bonds not long after publishing his pioneering article, "Portfolio Selection" in the prestigious *Journal of Finance*.

Following his own breakthroughs, we would have expected him to make elaborate calculations based on historical averages to find the optimal trade-off between risk and return. Dr. Markowitz took a different tack:

"I visualized my grief if the stock market went way up and I wasn't in it, . . . or if it went way down and I was completely in it. My intention was to minimize my future regret. So, I split my contributions 50/50 between bonds and equities."

CHAPTER 5 SUMMARY

- Whether the market is behaving well or poorly, expect a change in direction.

- The only reasonable investment is a long-term investment.

CHAPTER 6

THE MOST CRITICAL FOUR STEPS IN PLANNING

Lovers must love, singers must sing, and market analysts must predict the stock market. The main difference we can find is that loving and singing make people happy, while predicting the markets ultimately makes people poor and, thereafter, unhappy.

If you think you or anybody can accurately predict market movements, we suggest you take a look at the December 2008 issue of *Barron*. *Barron's* convened a dozen experts (market analysts) and asked them to forecast the S&P 500 index at the end of 2009. The predictions were all positive—which sounds like maybe they know what they're talking about, because they all agreed. But then the fun really amps up. Their forecasts (guesses) ranged from an increase of 5% to an increase of 38%. The median forecast (speculation) was 13%.

Give me a break. How can anybody take any prediction about the markets seriously when a panel of well-educated, well-informed professional market analysts can't get any closer than that?

Year after year such predictions are issued, and year after year the majority of predictions are far off the mark—as they were that year.

Do you think your predictions will be more accurate than the experts? At Warburton Capital, we sometimes get to thinking we can predict what the market will do, but we quickly dismiss our musings as delusional. We certainly won't wager our clients or our personal financial futures on speculation. We prefer to engage with the probable.

When it comes to selecting stocks, the probability of success is no greater than predicting market movements. Vegas offers better odds. Year after year, the vast majority of mutual funds managed by asset class specialists armed with volumes of fundamental and technical research fail to match the performance of their unmanaged index benchmarks.

Some people think they can pick winning stocks because they read the *Wall Street Journal* or watch CNBC. Whoa! Do we expect to find undiscovered secrets on the front page of the *Journal* or from Jim Cramer?

I've also met folks who take stock picking more seriously and have read a few books that "guarantee" market-beating performance. Hey, I've read about 200 books on how to play golf like the pros. How do you think that worked out? (It didn't, and it wasn't for lack of effort.)

Arguing with the market may be fun, but it's just not profitable. The designers of 401(k)plans will laugh out loud with stories about well-educated executive market timers and stock pickers who generate returns significantly inferior to the broad market year after year, yet refuse to curb their insanity.

As financial advisors, we often encounter people who say, "I have never made any money in the stock market." Without fail, naysayers have been guilty of the two cardinal sins I've discussed previously:

1) Market timing, and

2) Stock picking (inadequate diversification).

Given all the uncertainty, the inability to predict the "black swans" (the occurrence of highly improbable events), and the clear need to accumulate liquid net worth to permit a comfortable retirement, what is a person to do?

The answer is situationally specific planning.

1. Identify your needs.

2. Establish your goal.

3. Design your plan for liquid net worth accumulation and subsequent annuitization.

4.   Anticipate the uncertainty of capital markets.

How do you do that?

First, identify your needs. Figure out how much you spend. Accurately determine your lifestyle burn rate. Take a Saturday afternoon and figure out how much you spend on occupancy, cars, food, entertainment, insurance, and other expenditures that you view as necessary.

Second, establish your goal. Figure out how much liquid net worth you need to accumulate to sustain the funding of your lifestyle burn rate.

Third, design your plan. Figure out how you are going to accumulate liquid net worth throughout your working career and annuitize that liquid net worth throughout your retirement.

Fourth, anticipate the uncertainty of capital markets. Recognize the risk and return characteristics of the four fundamental investment vehicles:

a)   Cash or cash variants

b)   Bonds

c)   Stocks

d)   Private equity

Be realistic about how these investment vehicles perform if you invest in them properly (emphasis on "properly") and, thereby, successfully capture the expected risk and return characteristics of the asset class.

	PRINCIPAL STABILITY	LONG-TERM RETURNS	DAILY LIQUIDITY
CASH	Excellent	Inferior To Inflation	Yes
BONDS	Fair	Better Than Cash	Yes
STOCKS	Poor	Better Than Bonds	Yes
PRIVATE EQUITY	Horrid	Better Than Stocks	No

The critical planning steps outline a disciplined approach for increasing the probability to accumulate and not outlive your money. It is a risky world that we live in, and the word "guarantee" should be used with extreme caution. Risk and return are correlated. "Black swans" come out of nowhere. Conservative strategies and conservative assumptions should govern every decision.

We encourage every person on this planet with any financial means to take responsibility for their financial future.

- Get started now.

- Have a systematic investment plan.

- Or, if you are already retired, have a systematic annuitization plan

Failure to launch and failure to plan can only be blamed on the person in the mirror. It's easy, but unproductive, to blame a magazine, demands on time, or bad luck. In the final analysis, each of us is responsible for his or her own financial future.

If you are like Bob Vila and like to do it yourself, then do it. But be armed with knowledge and don't delude yourself with unrealistic expectations.

If you like the idea of objective advice, seek out a financial advisor. There are a number of highly qualified earnest stewards who have made this type of planning their life's work Avoid the "cowboys selling shiny things."

In closing, your financial plan should be grounded in the probable. Life is a matter of probabilities. Every time a person selects food to eat, the consequences of the food's impact on health is present. When we drive a car, there is a small but measurable probability of becoming involved in an accident.

Know what is probable and cast your fate to the probable. After all, the probable is what normally happens!

Chapter 6 Summary

- Rather than attempting to predict future market moves, engage with the probable.

- The two cardinal sins are market timing and stock picking.

- Planning leads to rational thinking and execution.

- Seek a financial planner who understands planning.

CHAPTER 7

WHY IS THE MARKET DOING
WHAT IT IS DOING?

"The well-reasoned long-term investing experience is usually positive. The short-term experience, no matter how well reasoned, is often times negative."—Charles Ellis, paraphrased from his 1985 classic, Investment Policy

One day after the Dow Jones 30 Industrials had closed –299 points (–4.24%), a buddy came into our office and cried, "Man, have you ever seen selling like this?"

As it develops, our buddy was a college student when the market closed –508 points (–22.6%) on Black Monday, October 19, 1987, so we will forgive him for not remembering an event that happened in an era when he was probably more interested in beer and the opposite sex.

Let's think about market action for a bit.

- How do we explain what's going on in the market when there is mass selling?

- Is it panic selling?

- Is the selling rational?

- Are public companies, in aggregate, genuinely that much less valuable as they were 15 months ago?

- Is the selling motivated by investors forced to liquidate to satisfy obligations?

- Are margin calls flushing weak investors out of the system?

- Are there any more sellers?

- Have we seen a selling capitulation?

- Who is buying?

- Why are those people buying?

These are all great questions for which there is no simple answer. The genuine value of companies rarely changes overnight to the positive or to the negative. Fear and greed drive stock prices over the short-term, and earnings growth drives stock prices over the long haul.

Clearly, our economy has been sorting out challenges of a magnitude that only occurs every 30–40 years. History shows us that we humans have been able to overcome anything that has been thrown at us in the past, just as we will overcome the challenges of this modern era. What will it take for our triumph?

It's the obvious stuff—including time and a lot of teamwork.

In our view, the stock and bond markets are functioning correctly. Willing sellers are being met by willing buyers in an orderly marketplace.

Some investors are buying or selling because they believe in one of the two great fictions:

- Market timing

- Stock picking

In spite of overwhelming evidence to the contrary, many investors believe they can predict market inflection points (market timing) or pick winning stocks (stock picking).Investors receive lots of encouragement from Wall Street brokerage firms that thrive on stock trading commissions and internal fees generated by their structured products.

Let's just admit it—whether buying or selling, we are embracing risk. Even when properly executed, investing is risky. Risk is substantially increased by engagement in activities that are destined to fail. Market timing and stock picking are destined to fail.

We view planning and well-reasoned investing as the only defense in a bear market, the only offense in a bull market, and the best way to mitigate risk. Reasonable investors have a plan and are buying or selling because it makes sense and not because of a market view that may or may not work out.

We view the development of a plan as essential to success in any endeavor, including investing.

If you save enough—work will be optional.

If you manage your investments properly—work will remain optional.

Any good plan will have financial practicalities as its foundation. A good plan will recognize needs, goals, and values, as well as how many years we have remaining until we can depend upon "mailbox income." Advanced planning will consider issues beyond our portfolio and include estate planning, tax mitigation, asset protection and charitable interests.

When investors focus their attention on long-term needs, goals and values and use that information to design a plan, the monthly value of stock/bond portfolios, as well as the current economic environment, becomes easier to tolerate.

If we have cash and the plan dictates accumulation of stocks, then by all means continue to invest regularly in global equities and try not to get overly excited about the great bargains you are scooping up.

If you need cash and the plan failed to identify this need, then by all means join those investors who are forced to sell and resolve to not get into such a position again.

Chapter 7 Summary

- The genuine value of companies rarely changes overnight to the positive or to the negative.

- Earnings growth drives stock prices over the long term.

- If you save enough—work will be optional.

- If you manage your investments properly—work will remain optional.

CHAPTER 8

CONEY DOG CHAT

Somewhere around the first of March 2009, one of my best buddies walked into my office en route to our appointed lunch (hot dogs smothered in chili at Terri's Coney Islander). He stated, with justifiable concern given the overwhelmingly negative financial news, "I just want to get out of the market until things calm down. Then, I'll get back in."

This set me off on one of my favorite sermons: The Concentrated Nature of Returns.

Over the history of recorded data, stock markets have demonstrated a capacity to make very abrupt moves in a very short time.

If we missed the best buying day every year over the past 80 years, returns would have gone from very attractive to not so good.

Data suggest that nobody knows in advance when the market has calmed down and nobody knows when the market will change direction. The only strategy that makes sense is to have a purposeful portion of our liquid net worth in stocks for long-term growth and a similarly purposeful portion of our liquid net worth safely in bonds for long-term safety.

Well, my Coney Dog buddy determined that he did have enough money in bonds to sustain him for almost a decade of lifestyle expense, so he decided to stay the course with his asset allocation and we wandered off to ingest more Coney Dogs.

Now, I'm not taking any credit for forecasting the market, but what a difference the subsequent two months made! The S&P 500 was up over 37% since the market low in March . Did that really represent the whole story? Heck no!

The following chart represents how each of the funds we utilize in our clients' equity portfolios performed over the March 9 through May 8, 2009 time period:

Despite an avalanche of negative economic news, global stock prices moved dramatically higher. Bizarre? No! This has happened before and will happen again, because economic news and market movements aren't highly correlated.

Now, let's not celebrate the beginning of a new bull market. Let's just recognize that the dramatic recovery over those two months offers a powerful illustration of the unpredictable and concentrated nature of stock returns.

Trading Symbol	Security Description	% Change 3/9/2009 to 5/8/2009
DFREX	Real Estate Securities Portfolio	57.5%
DFCEX	Emerging Markets Core Equity Portfolio	56.4%
DFGEX	Global Real Estate Securities Portfolio	54.1%
DFTWX	TA World ex US Core Equity Portfolio	52.0%
DFIEX	International Core Equity Portfolio	49.5%
DFQTX	US Core Equity 2 Portfolio	48.3%
DFTCX	TA US Core Equity 2 Portfolio	47.5%
	S&P 500	37.4%

If we aren't going to celebrate the next bull market, then, what are we going to do?

My suggestion = Get your asset allocation in order!

Assess your financial resources, obligations, goals, and needs. Armed with this information, create a plan to accumulate—in the most conservative manner possible—sufficient liquid net worth to make work optional.

And now, one more Coney Dog for the road.

A well-educated young man who worked for a prominent Wall Street firm appeared soon after on CNBC. He made a statement that his great investment idea was to invest in technology. Shortly thereafter, another well-educated young man who worked for a similarly prominent Wall Street Firm came on and stated, "The tech opportunity has come and gone and it's time to rotate into blah blah." Contradictions are continuous and certain in this business.

As I drove to work, it hit me. Wall Street firms represent that they offer great investment ideas for right now, yet if enough firms gather in a room, disagreement will certainly erupt concerning the great and the awful.

It seems reasonable to me to conclude that none of these folks or firms really know what they are talking about. They are all speculating. They all attempt to lure investors to become clients by the appearance of knowing something that will make clients a bunch of money quickly.

Thinking that it is possible to pick winning stocks contradicts objective academic research. Statistically significant data leads one to conclude that short-term security prices are random and the best estimate of a security's true value is the price it is trading at today.

Unlike the Wall Street gurus, we know that we have no idea which stocks will perform best over the next few months.

On the other hand, we believe we know very well which investments will probably do best over the longer-term:

- Stocks will probably out-perform bonds.

- Small cap stocks will probably out-perform large cap stocks.

- Value stocks will probably out-perform growth stocks.

More importantly—and without regard to Wall Street's lunacy or academic research—we believe that attempting to identify great investment ideas right now misses the most important point: How should we invest to achieve financial goals?

Once this light bulb goes off and investors focus on the important issue of achieving financial goals, the interest in Wall Street's great ideas is destined to fade.

What you should invest in right now has everything to do with your values, goals, needs, resources, and obligations. It has nothing to do with great ideas or the musings of Jim Cramer and/or Maria Bartiromo.

CHAPTER 8 SUMMARY

- Have a purposeful portion of liquid net worth in stocks for long-term growth.

- Have a similarly purposeful portion of net worth in bonds for long term safety.

- Bring order to asset allocation.

- Unlike Wall Street self-anointed gurus, we are well aware we have no idea which stocks will perform best over the next few months.

CHAPTER 9

LEO'S DISAPPOINTMENT

One Saturday morning I had a very early flight from Los Angeles to Tulsa and was fortunate to be seated next to a gentleman by the name of Leo Williams. Leo had been a world-class high jumper, who, at age 23, cleared 7'6" and won three NCAA titles. Leo's career did not culminate in the Olympic gold medal he seemed destined for, but instead, his best showing in the Olympic trials was in 1984 when he finished in fourth place and was awarded first-alternate status.

Lesser men might have responded with depression, but not Leo. Leo set about becoming a world-class advisor to physicians requiring specialized medical devices. Today, Leo owns his own firm, and is very enthusiastic about his family and the bright future ahead of him.

As I thought about Leo's Olympic disappointment, I was struck by the parallels of investors' hopes being crushed by the cataclysmic stock market of 2008.

What were we to do? Wallow in disappointment and grief? Or, perhaps we should have, like Leo, gotten up, dusted ourselves off, and went on with making the most of our lives.

It's certain the odds of investors being successful in the future are very high. Consider the following history and data.

Starting with the crash of October 1928, the stock market, as measured by the S&P 500, has delivered average annual returns of 9% per year. But averages can be misleading. There have been extended periods when returns finished well below (and well above) that mark.

We identify a muted return market as one that delivers an average annual return of 5% or below over a 10-year period. Since October 1929, muted return markets have occurred in 91 out of a possible 715 rolling 10-year periods. Recent market behavior has landed within that low standard by returning an average of –3% over the last 10 years.

On the bright side, muted markets have historically been followed by 10-year periods of strong returns. As the following chart indicates, since October 1929 the average annual return in the 10-year period following a muted market has been approximately 15%, with none returning less than 8%.

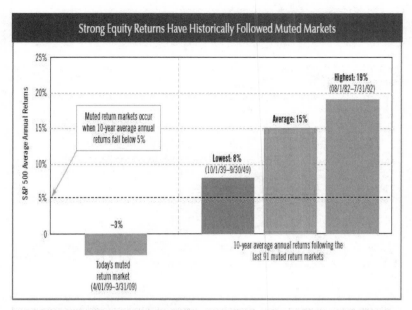

Strong Equity Returns Have Historically Followed Muted Markets

Muted return markets occur when 10-year average annual returns fall below 5%

Today's muted return market (4/01/99–3/31/09): –3%

10-year average annual returns following the last 91 muted return markets:
- Lowest: 8% (10/1/39–9/30/49)
- Average: 15%
- Highest: 19% (08/1/82–7/31/92)

Source: Ibbotson Associates. The S&P Index is a weighted, unmanaged index composed of 500 large-cap stocks. It provides a broad indicator of stock price movements. The performance above does not reflect the impact of taxes, management fees or sales charges. Investors cannot invest directly in an index.

The charts below show how markets have behaved in three of the 91 muted markets since October 1929. In each case, after 10 years of muted returns, the next 10 years were significantly more rewarding.

Clearly, the preceding information is simplistic and myopic. What about small cap indices? What about value indices? Although the precise numbers vary, the message is the same.

- Market returns revert to the mean.

- Periods of underperformance are generally followed by periods of outperformance.

- Periods of outperformance are generally followed by periods of underperformance.

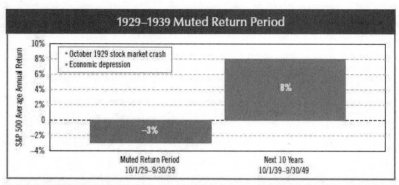

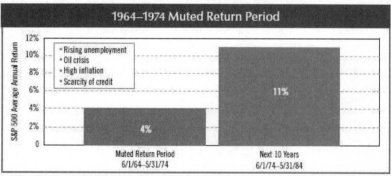

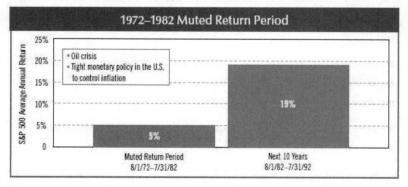

The word "generally" can create a predicament. Generally is not the same as always.

In our view, all investors benefit from maintaining a long-term perspective. Nobody knows when the market may move up or move down. Maintaining a long-term perspective increases the odds of an investor replacing the word "generally" with the word "probably."

While maintain a long-term perspective, we believe investors need to continually re-evaluate their needs, goals, resources, and obligations. Based on that evaluation and re-evaluation, the objective is to develop and modify (when your situation changes) a plan that will probably succeed and make work optional.

Notwithstanding the uncertainty of the markets and the tedious nature of planning, if history repeats itself, we are probably being set up for better times ahead.

NOTE: Jennison Dryden studied monthly rolling 10-year periods, starting in October 1929 and covering 715 monthly periods, to determine the frequency of muted return markets and the magnitude of returns during and after those markets. A "muted return market" is defined as one that delivers an average annual return of 5% or below over a 10-year period. Since October 1929, muted return markets have occurred in 91 out of a possible 715 rolling 10-year periods. The first period studied was October 1, 1929, through September 30, 1939, and the subsequent 10-year periods ranging from October 1, 1939 through September 30, 1949. The last period studied was April 1, 1989, through March 31, 1999, and the subsequent 10-year period ranging from April 1, 1999, through March 31, 2009.

Chapter 9 Summary

- The probability of a patient long-term equity investor being rewarded with attractive returns is high.

- Market returns revert to the mean.

- Periods of performance are cyclical.

CHAPTER 10

THE LOST DECADE

There are a number of articles circulating the industry which offer this thesis: 2000–2010 was a lost decade for investors because bonds out-performed stocks.

Is this fact or fiction? Well, it's kind of true—but it's mostly something that came out of the south end of a northbound horse!

Let's consider simplistic data that might have led to the errant propagation.

In this analysis, the thesis is accurate. If an investor had invested solely in one-month treasuries (bonds) or the S&P 500 (stocks), then bonds did outperform stocks.

Is that enough evidence to draw a conclusion? Did bonds outperform stocks last decade? Let's look at more comprehensive data.

One-Month U.S. Treasury Bills versus the S&P 500 Index

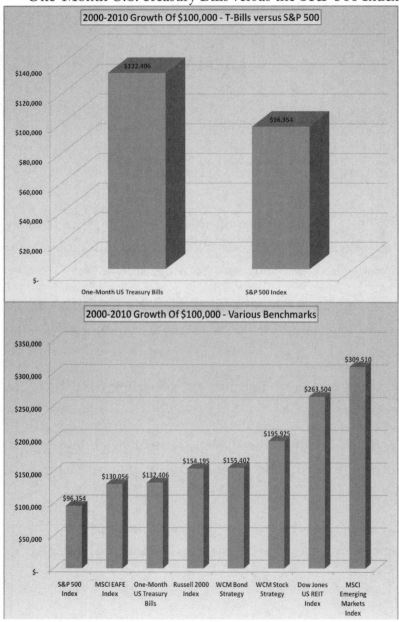

The growth of $100,000 invested at the beginning of the decade in one-month U.S. treasury bills was outpaced by investing in the Warburton Model Portfolios (either bonds or stocks) and several other stock indices as follows:

- $154,195 The Russell 2000 (US Small Cap) Index

- $155,042 The Warburton Bond Strategy

- $195,925 The Warburton Stock Strategy

- $263,504 The Dow Jones U.S. Real Estate Investment Trust (REIT) Index

- $309,510 The MSCI Emerging Markets (Non-Developed Countries) Index

What do we conclude from this?

Often times the analysis published by the financial press is simplistic, misleading, alarmist and useless.

We sympathize with investors disappointed by the returns of their stock market investments over the past decade. That said, we think we know what happened to those investors:

- They picked individual stocks, or somebody else picked stocks for them.

- They practiced market timing, or somebody else tried to time the market for them.

Neither stock picking nor market timing is dependable and will likely result in performance inferior to that which is obtainable by investing with the benefit of financial science and broadly diversified global portfolios.

Would you like to avoid a "lost decade"? We offer an alternative—utilize financial science and abandon the stock picking and market timing speculations recommended by traditional wealth management firms.

If you want to minimize the chance of a lost decade, call us. Neither we nor anyone else knows if bonds or stocks will be the superior investment over the next decade, but we do know that the application of financial science stacks the odds in our favor.

In closing, my sister Dr. Mary Ann Norfleet sent me an "old saying with a different twist."

> *"It is fruitless to become lachrymose*
> *over precipitately departed lacteal fluid."*

In other words, "Don't cry over spilled milk." There is wisdom in such sage advice to investors who suffered a lost decade. We urge moving on with purposeful investing grounded in financial science.

CHAPTER 11

THIS TOO, SHALL PASS

In the words of John Allen Paulos, professor of mathematics at Temple University and versatile author of books on a wide range of philosophical topics:

"Uncertainty is the only certainty there is, and knowing how to live with insecurity is the only security."

Seasoned observers of financial markets and capital market investors know that a predisposition to worry about one thing or another is instinctual. What's not often apparent is how quickly worries are factored into security prices and how rapidly the narrative changes.

Recent fretting points for investors include default risk in southern Europe, the threat of China's economy over-heating, the dependency of risk assets on government stimulus, and the implications of proposed regulatory reforms in the healthcare and banking industries.

A fair observation for the majority of hot-button financial and economic issues is that by the time you read about them in newspapers and magazines, the markets have moved onto worrying about something else.

Consider Greece as an excellent example. A search of *Bloomberg* for the words "Greece and default" yielded nearly 300 news stories in the month of March 2010. The subject of articles ranged from the "ying" (fears of outright default) to, by the end of the month, the "yang" (news of a strengthening euro as Greek fears receded).

If one searched *Bloomberg* for "stimulus," more than 600 news articles appeared in March 2010, ranging from Brazil's attempt to lure investors with governmental stimulus (infrastructure spending) to news that Japan's retail sales were growing at their fastest pace in 13 years, thanks partly to government stimulus.

Today we benefit from, and are sometimes cursed by, rapid global information flows. Aided by web-based distribution, news is incorporated into security prices almost instantly. A geopolitical development like a bomb blast in a Moscow subway, economic news such as an agreement on a bailout for Greece, or company-specific news like a Chinese firm buying Volvo from Ford all find their way into prices before the average person is aware they have occurred.

Wall Street reflects the news in pricing long before the average investor gains any knowledge of the events.

Is it a surprise to know that investors err by tinkering with their portfolios based on information that is already reflected into securities pricing? This type of investing behavior is like trying to catch a falling sword.

A more useful approach is to accept that markets are extremely efficient at incorporating fresh information into prices and that trying to second guess how the markets will react to today's news is hazardous to your wealth.

An Australian financial advisor developed a useful technique for dealing with queries from clients regarding their portfolios and the capital market implications of whatever issue is currently dominating the financial media headlines: "To be completely honest, I don't know what the implications are. But I can tell you this: *it won't last*. Now let's talk about *your* news."

This is a healthy approach to responding to news that dominates the markets. Be concerned with personal values, goals, needs, resources, and obligations. Make changes when your personal situation changes and ignore "the noise."

The economy, headlines, and governmental policy are topical and forever changing. However, remain mindful—external issues are beyond our control. If our portfolios are purposefully constructed, news of the day does not necessitate action.

CHAPTER 12

STOP LOSS STRATEGY

The DOW plunged about 1,000 points during intraday trading on Thursday, May 6, 2010, then recovered over 650 points and closed down 347 points (3%) for the day.

It appears there was a trading error (now being referred to as the "Fat Finger Trade") that caused accelerated selling and contributed to the steep temporary decline.

Proctor and Gamble's stock price dropped from an opening price of 61.91 to an intraday low of 39.37 in minutes(a drop of 36%). Speculation exists that the sudden price drop was a trading error. The sudden price drop triggered incremental program (computer-based) trading to occur—this happens automatically when a stock or index hits a certain price. The increased selling drove the price (and other prices)lower, causing other computer-based trading to execute sells, resulting in further price decrease. After the drop to $39, the stock quickly rebounded to around $60 and closed down only 2% for the day.

The above referenced Proctor and Gamble scenario inspires us to make a comment on utilizing a "stop loss" strategy. (A stop loss is an order to sell a security if it trades at a specified price below the current market price.) We don't believe in trading strategies of any type. We view trading as gambling in the stock market, and have not been presented with any evidence to suggest that the majority of traders consistently make money. Luck may carry the day for a few…the vast majority will lose big time!

That said, the intraday market volatility caused us to question the wisdom of utilizing stop losses. That day was a clear example of a situation where a trader might have had a stop loss set under a stock only to see the stop loss executed before the security rallied substantially a few minutes later. Clearly, selling at the bottom is a tactical reality that is hazardous to investor wealth.

If there is an abnormal event such as a trade error causing increased volatility, be aware of it, and frame the current event in the proper perspective.

There is always noise in the market.

That noise contributes to emotional distress and volatility.

Volatility creates the risk and return from which we may benefit as long-term investors in a globally diversified portfolio.

We would like to make a few comments about fixed income:

- The DFA fixed income funds our clients hold do not contain any sovereign debt of Portugal, Italy, or Greece (PIG), the sovereign domiciles at the center of recent market concerns.

- Going forward, PIG bonds may decline or rally.

- Any subsequent decline or rally of PIG bonds may impact the broad fixed income markets by influencing the emotions of market participants.

- Any subsequent decline or rally of PIG bonds may impact the broad fixed income markets by impacting the financial stability of investors owed money by the PIGs. We are pleased that our fixed income funds, by design, do not hold any PIG bonds.

CHAPTER 13

ADVICE AND ADVISORS

I'm often forced to opine on the "investment pornography" coming from the brokerage houses or from the mouths of the talking heads on CNBC or other outlets. One week was different—it seemed everyone wanted to talk about Goldman-Sachs and the Senate hearings.

The crux of the issue was proffered by Knut A. Rostad, chairman, Committee for the Fiduciary Standard. Consider this quote from *Wealth Manager*, "Goldman Sachs, Suitability and the Fiduciary Standard," April 21, 2010:

> *"The case highlights the wide gap and opposing roles of a broker who is permitted in law to further his and his firm's interests at the expense of customers, and a fiduciary who is required in law to put his clients' interests first. This is at the core of why the fiduciary standard is important."*

To hear Lloyd Blankfein, Goldman Sachs CEO, tell it, the financial markets did their job. Absent the unfortunate downturn in the housing market, everything would have been just fine.

In the heated Senate subcommittee hearing held on April 27, the Goldman CEO argued that Goldman sold people the risk exposures they wanted and were never obligated to disclose that the collateralized debt obligations (CDOs) they were packaging and selling to their clients were the very same investments they were betting against (selling short) in their own accounts.

So we get to the heart of the matter:

1. Did Goldman have the obligation to disclose their view to their clients?

2. Was Goldman wrong to sell investment vehicles they secretly and frequently cited in emails as being *garbage* (expletive deleted and replaced)?

3. Did Goldman break the law by not disclosing a conflict of interest—their negative view of products they were selling?

It's difficult to justify the corporate behavior that played into the downturn. Blankfein's $9 million bonus, in part the result of the *garbage* assets Goldman sold and shorted, is uniquely difficult to rationalize since it occurred in the same year that millions of Americans lost their jobs and their homes.

Again, at the heart of this matter is what are Goldman Sachs, JP Morgan, Merrill Lynch, Wells Fargo, Smith Barney, Edward D. Jones, AG Edwards, Charles Schwab, eTrade, and dozens of other brokerage firms permitted to do under the standard of suitability?

The SEC asserted that Goldman's conduct was not permissible.

Blankfein vociferously disagreed.

The outcome may rely on answering this question:

Is selling a garbage investment illegal or just immoral?

If the SEC determines the practice to be illegal, Goldman and the other brokerage houses have a big problem. If the practice is judged immoral, investors have a big problem.

There is a solution: Seek the advice of a fiduciary.

Fiduciaries are required to act with undivided loyalty to their clients. They are required to disclose how they get paid and reveal any corresponding conflicts of interest.

Knut Rostad's Committee for the Fiduciary Standard states the five principles of fiduciary standard, as follows:

1. Put the client's best interest first.

2. Act with prudence; that is, with the skill, care, diligence, and good judgment of a professional.

3.   Do not mislead clients; provide conspicuous, full, and fair disclosure of important facts.

4.   Avoid conflicts of interest.

5.   Fully disclose and fairly manage, in the client's favor, unavoidable conflicts.

The standards are noble aspirations that many brokerage houses would like investors to believe are followed—at least until the firms are pressed on the issue, as Blankfein was in his January 2010 SEC hearing. He stated, "We are not a fiduciary." He added that Goldman must "fully disclose what an instrument is and be honest in our dealings, but we are not managing somebody else's money."

Unlike a brokerage firm, Warburton Capital is a fiduciary. We manage our clients' assets. We willingly accept the responsibility to put our clients' best interests above our own. We make investment recommendations that are in the best interests of our clients and their ability to take on bond or stock market risk.

At Warburton Capital we accept this fiduciary obligation. We receive no revenue sharing and no incentives to recommend one mutual fund or investment over another.

If there is one fundamental lesson that investors can learn from the recent Senate Subcommittee meeting, it is this:

*Work with a fiduciary who accepts the fiduciary responsi-
bility and puts your best interests above their own.*

CHAPTER 14

ACTIVE VERSUS PASSIVE

Once I was approached by a nationally prominent publisher who serves the financial advisor community and asked to submit an article for publication.

This was a unique opportunity for me to speak to my colleagues and promote that which I believe. Helping our clients achieve their goals is our number one priority. The preferred tools of traditional money managers (stock picking and market timing) are worthless.

Following is the article I submitted. If you can read this through the eyes of a financial advisor, it might give you a few useful insights about our industry.

TRADITIONAL MONEY MANAGER BLAH BLAH

Most of us who have survived and thrived in the money management industry were trained under the traditional model of getting in front of somebody and making a pitch. Our pitch was designed to make us look smart and normally started out with something like "our best idea right now is blah blah."

Thanks to our persistence and personal charisma, we succeeded in winning a few clients, who referred more clients, and ultimately created a book of business from which we could make a living. So off we went with more "best ideas right now" and more "blah blah."

Over the years, my clients and I heard countless presentations about "our best idea right now" and "blah blah" from active managers (sector rotators, asset class rotators, market timers, and stock pickers) who had been recently (i.e., temporarily) successful in predicting or outperforming the market but soon (i.e. inevitably) lost their touch.

As expected, a few of our clients, motivated by their faith in us and the prospect of outsized returns, lapped up the pabulum and entrusted their money to our recommended active managers.

After some reasonable period of time, without fail, the performance of our recommended active managers reverted to sub-median, and my firm and I were on the road with a new cadre of active managers and their new version of "blah blah."We apologized for the mediocre performance of our old managers and proselytized that we had found new active managers with "better ideas right now."

It didn't take me long to figure out that I didn't want to be part of this.

Armed with my computer, an Internet connection, and Google, I set out to see if there was actually any science to the wealth management industry. Well—seek and ye shall find. Yes, there is a wealth of science pointing the way toward strategies that make sense.

Of course, it wasn't a brief research project. Before I found the science, I found a lot more "blah blah." An example that sticks in my mind was "continental bias." The majority of U.S. money managers recommend that the bulk of their client assets be invested in U.S. equity markets with smaller allocations off continent. The majority of European money managers recommend that the bulk of their client assets be invested in Europe with smaller allocations off continent to the U.S. and Asia. Similarly, Asian money managers recommend major allocations to Asia with minority allocations to the U.S. and Europe. Gimme a break. Where is the science in this?

Continuing my independent research, I stumbled across the efficient market hypothesis. This theory, primarily attributed to Nobel laureate Professor Eugene Fama of the University of Chicago, postulates that it is impossible to beat the market with clever security selection because prices already incorporate and reflect all relevant information. The practical application of this theory is that nobody can pick stocks that will outperform their peer group. For an irrefutable example of the inability of stock pickers to predict future information, and thereby future prices, one need look no farther than British Petroleum (BP).

Over the past decade BP was lauded for their proven reserves and their ongoing expansion of those reserves. Gosh, how is BP looking right now? Is their balance sheet even strong enough to avert bankruptcy, let alone should a cautious investor buy their shares? It was pretty hard to predict that oil spill!

Although the efficient market hypothesis has non-believers, I have found no statistically significant evidence to refute it. In fact, significant data has been presented by and exists within the databases of CRSP, SPIVA, Morningstar, and others to support it. The likelihood of any stock or bond picker outperforming a relevant benchmark is not good over the short term and decreases over longer periods. It is for good reason that the Third Restatement of the Prudent Investor Act directs fiduciaries to utilize a passive strategy.

So, let's presume you can't pick stocks and move onto another form of active management. How about market timing?

Is it possible to figure out when to move between the stock market and cash? Mark Hulbert, the publisher of the *Hulbert Financial Digest*, has compiled the most comprehensive data I have seen on market timers, which has led this observer to conclude that the chances of generating out-sized returns are small, and the chances of grossly underperforming the relevant benchmark are high. Although I have never seen evidence as academic as Professor Fama's, I have had lengthy conversations with numerous well-educated market timers who have dedicated their careers to the discipline. Each of them has represented to me that the best you can hope for with market timing is to replicate the returns of a market index with less volatility and inferior tax efficiency.

So, let's presume market timing makes no sense either.

What is a financial advisor to do?

Well, I think the answer is clear—admit to your clients that neither you nor anybody else can cleverly pick stocks or market time. However, you have a more worthwhile objective—you can help your clients achieve their goals!

Represent to your clients that which is accurate. Utilize well-reasoned tools like purposeful asset dedication, purposeful asset allocation, and tax efficient asset location to stack the deck in the client's favor while we all allow the capital markets to deliver the performance that is probable.

Of course, inherent to my recommendation is that an advisor utilizes passive management—some form of indexing. This causes heartburn for many advisors and elicits comments like "How can I attract and retain clients utilizing anything that resembles indexing?" To this question I can only answer, "You would be surprised." Once your clients know that you understand their goals and have produced an investment plan that has a high likelihood of achieving those goals consistent with their values, resources, obligations, and needs, the clients will be pleased and you will be on the road to being their trusted advisor.

As advisors we have a choice: stand for a bunch of worthless "blah blah" by having a "best idea right now" and attempting to predict that which cannot be predicted, or stand for helping clients achieve their goals with financial science on our side.

The choice is easy for me. I won't bet my reputation or my client's financial goals on active management, any "best ideas right now," or any "blah blah."

CHAPTER 15

ONE THING

B ack in 1990, I had a buddy who was 43 years old and had just sold his company for $61,000,000. That is a lot of money today, but it was even more twenty-five years ago!

This buddy of mine was intense. One day we were talking about business, when he seemingly went into a trance. In a detached tone he whispered to me, "Tom, do you ever dream about sex?" Shocked, I (for once in my life) kept my mouth closed while he went on with his out of body monologue. "Tom, I haven't dreamt about sex in 20 years. Each night before I go to bed I sit in my thinking chair and I figure out the one really important thing I can do tomorrow to make a bunch of money. Then, I dream about that one thing, I get up in the morning, I do that one thing and, then," coming out of his trance and becoming playfully charming, "I just mess around for the rest of the day, talk on the phone, or walk around and chat with my staff."

Over the years I've thought about my buddy many times. I've thought about how bizarre his behavior was and the otherworldly focus he brought to his game.

Can you imagine the power of doing 365 really important things every year?

How many of us get up every day with great intentions but let the day get away from us in the frenzy of meetings, phone calls, mail, emails, and other distractions? Five o'clock rolls around, our energy level is starting to wane, the allure of our families beckon and we depart our place of work with the one really important thing undone. (My sister, the psychologist, says this is a pattern conflict labeled with a number of terms ranging from the interesting "approach avoidance" to the mundane "procrastination.")

At Warburton Capital we are in the business of helping our clients manage their wealth effectively by getting one really important thing done systematically until all of the ducks are lined up neatly in a row.

After thousands of meetings with clients, we've observed general themes to really important things and the ducks that need to be aligned.

- Wealth Preservation—To preserve wealth, it's imperative to hold a variety of investments that provide for immediate liquidity needs, emergency liquidity contingencies, and growth for retirement.

- Wealth Enhancement—To enhance wealth, it's essential to work with a CPA capable of assessing your tax liabilities well in advance of the perfunctory tax filing date so you can actually do something about it.

- Wealth Transfer—To transfer wealth efficiently, it's critical to work with an attorney who is an estate planning specialist comfortable beyond the basics of marital deduction trusts, pour-over wills, advanced directives, and the durable power of attorney.

- Wealth Protection—To protect wealth effectively, it's mandatory to work with an insurance professional who understands needs and provides solutions as opposed to a product pusher interested in selling an annuity to win a trip to Hawaii.

- Wealth Sharing—To share your wealth with earnest charities, it's important to work with professionals who deal with charities everyday and know which charities do the most good for their given beneficiaries.

To maximize the wealth management initiatives, we suggest spending time in a thinking chair. Prioritize issues before bed, and then dream about one thing all night. If thinking chairs and dreaming about one thing are not your cup of tea, consider Warburton Capital.

We are in the business of being your thinking chair. Through a consultative process, we get to know our clients, help them clarify their most important goals and values, quantify their needs, resources, and obligations and insure that really important things get done systematically until all the ducks are lined up neatly in a row.

Get that one thing done tomorrow—and every day until you achieve your goals!

CHAPTER 16

THE 24-HOUR RULE

Way back in 1990 (before the Internet), my wife—the lovely Miss Vicki—and I lived in Kansas City next door to Marty and Pat Schottenheimer. Marty was the head coach of the then pretty darn successful Kansas City Chiefs.

Living next door to Marty provided a number of unusual opportunities, not the least of which was learning about his coaching philosophies.

One of Marty's fundamental precepts was "The 24-Hour Rule," which went something like this:

- No matter what happens, we forget about it after 24 hours.

- If we win, we celebrate for 24 hours—then prepare for next week.

- If we lose, we grieve for 24 hours—then prepare for next week.

Marty's goal was to keep his team on an emotional even keel and remain mindful of the tasks that lie ahead.

I've thought about Marty's 24-Hour Rule many times over the past couple of decades and, most recently, how the rule can benefit investors.

The 24-Hour Rule allows investors to maintain an emotional even keel, remain mindful of realistic goals, and become neither overly excited or overly distraught by short-term market movements.

Does maintaining an even keel sound easy to you?

Let's review a few negative headlines and see if the boat begins to rock:

- "Dow Declines for a 5th Day"—*Wall Street Journal*, August 17, 2010

- "Homebuilder Confidence Sinks for 3rd Month"—AP, August 16, 2010

- Friday's Job Report: Forecast Is For More Disappointment"—CNBC, August 6, 2010

- "Asian Shares Sluggish Amid Global Growth Worries"—AP, August 16, 2010

Now, let's counter the preceding gloom with a few upbeat headlines:

- "Blue Chips Rose 7.1% in July, Best Stock Month in a Year"—*Wall Street Journal*, July 31, 2010

- "August Historically Has Been Surprisingly Good for Stocks"—*Market Watch*, August 2, 2010

- "Stocks Rise on Earnings, Economic Reports"—AP, August 17, 2010

- "Wednesday Look Ahead: Stocks, Bonds Could See Follow-Through Wednesday"—CNBC, August 17, 2010

What do we realistically expect the global equity markets to do?

How about this: "Unpredictable Daily, Weekly, Monthly, and Annual Fluctuations"?

If we realistically expect unpredictable fluctuations then why would we want to get overly excited about a recent advance or a recent decline? It would make better sense for us to invoke the 24-Hour Rule--celebrate briefly after an advance or grieve briefly after a decline—then get back to our daily business knowing that our race is not run and our game is not over for many years or even decades. (Of course, the preceding implies that our asset allocation is well-reasoned, we have sufficiently provided for our immediate and intermediate currency needs, and only invested in the stock market with our patient capital.)

At Warburton Capital, we subscribe fully to the 24-Hour Rule. When the markets are up we like it, but we don't allow ourselves to become intoxicated with self-confidence. Likewise, when the markets are down we don't like it, but we don't find ourselves irrationally depressed and running for the sell line.

In summary: We don't let our emotions, a few headlines, or a few days of market volatility influence our decision making. Long-term thinking is indifferent to short-term outcomes.

CHAPTER 17

WOMEN ARE BETTER INVESTORS THAN MEN

Last month I read an article by Eugene Fama, Jr.(vice president, Dimensional Fund Advisors), that I found informative. The article opened with this thesis:

> *"Here's a controversial thought:*
> *men and women are different."*

So I'm thinking, "I've known this since I was a teenager." But I read on to see if, perhaps, Gene Jr. missed junior high school.

"Men and women are different in how they invest!"

Amazingly, there is a large body of evidence in review of gender-based financial behavior.

Women tend to be very involved in family financial affairs.

- 60% of women manage the household checkbook.

- 58% pay the bills.

- 44% oversee the budget.[1]

[1]*Share Builder Women and Investing* survey, 2007.

So it looks like women do the bookkeeping. What am I missing here?

Only 15% of married women take primary care of the family investments!

The uncomfortable end to this story (sorry, guys) is the fact that:

When it comes to choosing investments,
women tend to be more diligent!

Surveys suggest:

- Men chase "hot" stocks and mutual funds.

- Women spend more time researching before investing.

How do we hope to explain this? Women are more cautious? Men are overly confident?

Although I won't speculate on the "why" of gender behavior, it appears that the female approach is superior. Academic observers Brad Barber and Terrance Odean find that though women hold less risky portfolios than men, after adjusting for differences in risk, women achieve bigger returns.

I am relieved to provide a gender-neutral observation: over-confident investors trade too much and do poorly.

Professors Barber and Odean go to great lengths to explain that "gender is but a convenient statistical tool," "a variable that provides a natural proxy" for the real factor at work which is over-confidence.

Researchers in psychology have long held that men are more prone to over-confidence. Over-confident investors trade more aggressively. Over-confidence results in increased trading expense and increased taxation, which in turn, reduces performance.

Professors Barber and Odean then set out to determine if the population that is naturally over-confident earns lower average returns than the population that isn't over-confident.

The professors analyzed a significant database of brokerage accounts from the 1990s. They found that married men trade 45% more than married women and earn annual risk-adjusted net returns that are 1.4% lower than women investors.

The differences widen when the sample consists of married investors:

- Single men trade 67% more than single women and earn annual risk-adjusted net returns of 2.3%.

- Single men have average portfolio turnover of 77% per year.

- Single women have average portfolio turnover around 53% per year.

(Note: Both of these turnover numbers are obscene. Turnover decreases tax efficiency. We like to see portfolio turnover at 10% per year or less.)

So, what's going on with gender-differentiated investing results?

- Men are raised to embrace competition and risk.

- Men like to race a lot and can't wait for the next competition.

- Research—guys don't like to ask for directions.

- Women are more likely to avoid knife-fights, scotch, or taking a flyer on some dicey stock or hedge fund.

- Women take their time before committing assets.

- Women are likely to seek out data and expert help.

- Multiple minds are better than one.

Speaking broadly, men are generally more amenable to taking the risks necessary to meet goals, and women are generally more amenable to mitigating the risks necessary to meet goals.

An objective third-party—a well-informed advisor—may be useful in helping risk takers and risk mitigators find well-reasoned common ground.

Investors enhance the probability of success by considering both expected return and expected risk. Multifactor investing recognizes that risk and return are related.

Investors that embrace multifactor investing—considering risk and return—are more inclined to structure purposeful portfolios and avoid the pitfalls of emotional trading.

Again, an objective third-party—a well-informed advisor—will spend at least as much time talking about risk as talking about return.

In every investment decision, a multifactor (risk and return) framework helps resolve the ancient conflict between the impulse to take risks and prudence. A combination of gender tendencies seems most prudent.

CHAPTER 18

RESOLVED

How's this for a New Year's Resolution? Repeat after me: "I resolve that I will abandon personal stock picking and I will not permit that foolishness to be foisted upon me by stock brokers, money managers, or financial advisors."

New evidence shows up every day suggesting that it makes more sense to invest in index funds than to personally pick stocks, invest in hedge funds, invest in actively managed mutual funds, or let a money manager pick stocks for you.

Of course, index funds don't look very appealing after a wretched year for stocks. However, the data in numerous studies indicates that after fees and taxes, the vast majority of hedge funds and actively managed funds fail to do better.

In the February 1, 2009, issue of *Economics & Portfolio Strategy* (a newsletter for institutional investors), Mark Kritzman pounded another stake in the hearts of stock pickers (i.e. active managers). Kritzman, who teaches a financial engineering course for graduate students at M.I.T.'s Sloan School of Management, analyzed the long-term impact of the expenses incurred—taxes, management fees, performance fees, and transaction costs—on hedge funds and actively managed fund performance.

This study sounds simple, but measuring these costs accurately is tedious. Performance is highly dependent on the sequence of taxes incurred and performance fees levied, all of which is triggered by the random sequence of positive and losing years.

Kritzman devised a method to take contingencies into account. He calculated the average return over a hypothetical 20-year period, net of all expenses, of three hypothetical investments: a stock index fund with an annualized return of 10%, an actively managed mutual fund with an annualized return of 13.5%,and a hedge fund with an annualized return of 19%. The volatility of the three funds' returns—along with turnover rates, transaction fees, management fees, and performance fees—was based on what he determined to be industry averages.

As is consistent with a vast number of other studies, Kritzman concluded that when performance was accurately measured net of fees and taxes, the winner was the index fund. After fees and taxes, the index fund's average return was 8.5% per year, versus 8%for the actively managed fund, and 7.7%for the hedge fund.

The hedge fund performance and actively managed fund performance were significantly impaired by taxes and expenses. Taxes and expenses ate up huge amounts of return—9 and 3.5 percentage points a year, respectively.

So, how much out-performance would a hedge fund or actively managed mutual have to produce to overcome the incremental taxes and expenses? Kritzman concluded that to break even with the index fund, the hedge fund would have to outperform the index fund by 10 points per year. The actively managed fund would have to outperform by an average of 4.3 percentage points per year.

Can that be done? How many actively managed mutual funds are able to out-perform the S&P 500 Index by at least four percentage points per year over a statistically significant period of time? There were 452 domestic equity mutual funds in the Morningstar database that existed continually for the 20 years through the time period Kritzman studied. Morningstar reported that just 13 of those funds beat the Standard & Poor's 500-stock index by at least four percentage points per year, on average, over that period. That's less than 3 out of every 100 funds—a virtual needle in a haystack.

Of course, figuring out who did well in the past is pretty easy. Figuring out who will do well in the future is darn near impossible. Let's not forget—past performance is not predictive of future performance. It's a well-known fact that very few funds that out-perform one year do well the next year.

Finance Professor Russell Wermers at the University of Maryland believes that it is exceedingly probable that any fund that has beaten the market by an average of more than one percentage point per year over the last decade achieved that return almost entirely due to luck alone.

So now we have the issue of luck versus skill. If 1,000 people went over Niagara Falls in a barrel, we'd expect one or two to survive. Will that be due to luck or skill? If 1,000,000 people buy lottery tickets, we expect that one or two will win. Will that be due to luck or skill? Stock picking works the same way. Investors are encouraged by unscrupulous, or perhaps uninformed, advisors to confuse luck with skill.

Kritzman believes the investment implications are clear:"It is very hard, if not impossible, to justify active management for investors if their goal is to grow wealth." He goes on to state, "Those who insist on an actively managed fund are almost certainly deluding themselves."

In tax-sheltered accounts, Kritzman concedes, the odds are relatively more favorable for active management, because, in his simulations, taxes accounted for about two-thirds of the expenses of the actively managed mutual fund and nearly half of the hedge funds. But he emphasizes the word "relatively." "Even in a tax-sheltered account," he says, "the odds of beating the index fund are still poor."

Consider this quote from Professor Meir Statman, the Glenn Klimek Professor of Finance in the Leavey School of Business at Santa Clara University:

"The house [casino] takes a cut on each spin of the wheel, paying out less in winnings than it collects in bets. So roulette is a negative-sum game, and so is your non-index mutual fund (actively managed fund)."

We all know our well-intentioned New Year's diet and exercise resolutions are likely to fade as January moves along. So, let's resolve to do something that overwhelming evidence suggests will be terrific for our long-term financial health.

Repeat after me: "I will abandon personal stock picking and I will not permit that foolishness to be foisted upon me by stock brokers, money managers, or financial advisors."

CHAPTER 19

FRET FREE

A life-long buddy came into my office. We exchanged pleasantries until the inevitable philosophizing began. We normally begin with complex issues like "What's the meaning of life?" and as the afternoon progresses we wallow in less mundane initiatives, such as "Why does my wife think I'm crazy?"

At a rare quiet moment, my buddy said he was living a fretless life.

A fretless life!

What a nice thought. This sounded ideal.

We agreed that his financial resources were such that he could quit work anytime he wanted. He made the comment that he knew he could quit anytime—but he likes his work and doesn't see any reason to quit.

Work is optional!

Does that sound terrific or what?

This is where the rubber meets the road for many of my friends and clients.

1. Now that I have enough money, what am I supposed to do with my time?

2. Now that I can do whatever I want, what do I want to do? Continue work as an avocation? Abandon my workplace cold turkey?

We observe transitions (both the slow wind-down and the cold turkey) from professional life to private life as very satisfying for the vast majority of our clients. I think a part of this satisfied mindset is derived because as more and more join retired folks in retirement, everybody thinks it's normal and okay to be retired.

Many of us get to a point where—no matter how passionate we were about our work—we're ready to relax.

We also observe that many of our clients in their seventies advise us that they hate vacations, and their ideal activity is puttering around the house.

As humans, we exhibit remarkably similar behavior at specific stages of our lives. Is this where we are all headed? A world where our ideal activity is puttering around the house?

Permit me to speculate: Probably! And that's just fine! If all we want to do is putter and we are able to putter, by all means we should do it!

Between now and then, how should we behave?

Maybe you are still grinding hard. Your goals have not been fulfilled or, perhaps you still need to push rocks up the hill.

Whichever is the case, let's resolve to achieve fretless status before we decide to putter. Let's resolve to at some point in the future be living a fretless life.

How do we do that?

Well, we talk with folks about money all the time. This is pretty much what we've observed as an action plan for a fretless life:

1.   Live within your means.

2.   Save before you consume.

3.   Save money systematically.

4.   Set-up an automated saving plan.

5.   The more you can save the better.

6.   Borrow money strategically, if at all.

Good Debt:

1.   Education

2. Buying a business

3. Buying a home

Bad Debt:

1. Anything else *(absent extremely attractive terms)*

It's really that simple. The above outline guarantees that no matter how much you make you will save something and your wealth accumulation will not be impaired by debt for lifestyle.

My fretless buddy incorporated many of the above principals into his life. Now, as long as he continues to know what he likes to do with his time or he acquires an affinity for puttering, his life will be perfect!

He planned it to be just the way it is.

CHAPTER 20

SEVEN HEADLINES TO BEAT THE GLOOM

If we've had a chance to visit with you either lately or ever, you know that we believe in capturing the returns of global capitalism.

Sure, the sovereign debt (government debt) situation looks bleak in many countries. We have to ask:

"Are we depending on governments for our future prosperity, or are we depending on free enterprise capitalism?"

It may be interesting to note that there are many prominent firms in Japan that have prospered in spite of two atomic bombs essentially destroying their country. Further, there are even more prominent firms in Germany that have prospered in spite of two World Wars that destroyed infrastructure.

Do companies outlive governments?

We're concerned about governments enduring, but we are more concerned about global free enterprise capitalism enduring!

If global free enterprise capitalism collapses, where is the safe haven?

Sovereign debt is overwhelming throughout the world, but global free enterprise capitalism isn't a sad story.

We all know that the financial press spends a lot of time fire-hosing each of us with negative news. Global free enterprise capitalism is not in horrid shape. Here are some headlines from 2011:

- "Robust Growth in Germany Pushes Prices"— Analysts see a strong chance that German inflation will head towards 3% by the end of the year against a backdrop of robust growth in Europe's biggest economy (Reuters, July, 27, 2011).

- "Brazil Domestic Demand Still Strong"—The Economist Intelligence Unit says economic growth in Brazil surprisingly picked up speed in the first quarter, challenging the government's efforts to cool the expansion (EIU, July 6, 2011).

- "Japan: Retail Sales Top Estimates"—Japan's retail sales rose 1.1% in June 2011, exceeding all economists' forecasts and adding to signs the economy is bouncing back from an initial post-disaster plunge (*Bloomberg*, July 28, 2011).

- "No Fear in China"—Traders betting on gains in China's biggest companies are pushing options prices to the most bullish level in two years. The Chinese economy is projected to grow by 9.4%in 2011 (*Bloomberg*, July 28, 2011).

- "Southeast Asia Booms"—Southeast Asian markets are the world's top performers in 2011 thanks to strong economic and corporate fundamentals. Thailand's index hit a 15-year high in July and Indonesia's a record high (Reuters, July 22, 2011).

- "Australian Boom Keeps Rate Rise on the Agenda"—The Australian dollar hit its highest level in 30 years in late July as traders looked to the prospect of another rise in interest rates on the back of a resource investment boom (*Wall Street Journal*, July 27, 2011).

- "New Zealand Bounces Back"—The New Zealand economy has grown more strongly than expected after the Christchurch earthquake, helped by improving terms of trade. The Reserve Bank signals it may raise interest rates (*Bloomberg*, July 28, 2011).

Standing back from all this, the picture that emerges of the world outside North America and southern Europe is of robust economic conditions. If anything, policymakers in many parts of the world, particularly in Asia, are seeking to pull back demand rather than stoke it.

Australia, for instance, enjoyed its best terms of trade in more than 50 years. An unprecedented investment boom in mining injected extraordinary wealth into the economy and helped to push the Australian dollar to levels not seen since it was floated in the early 1980s.Likewise, China, India, and much of Southeast Asia saw strong investment flows and seemed to be more about over-heating than anything else.

This is not to say that all is right with the world. The aftermath of the global financial crisis has created severe problems, particularly in terms of public sector debt and deficits. But we know that that news is in the price. Meanwhile, economic activity in much of the world is thriving.

For equity investors, this means opportunities for wealth building are increasing, not decreasing. Moreover, the global economy is becoming multi-polar, rather than overly dependent on the United States, which means the potential benefits from broad diversification are even greater.

That's why focusing too much on the day-to-day headlines with the U.S. debt ceiling or European sovereign issues risks missing many of the good stories out there.

Of course and as always, we are not recommending that the stock market(s) are where you should have all of your money. There's more to the story than finding great investments.

We believe in purposeful allocations to stocks/bonds in proportions that make sense for the unique economic complexity that defines you.

Have some cash; own some bonds; own some stocks; own some private deals; own some life insurance—each has its place in a thoughtful plan.

We'll close this chapter with this thought from Nobel Laureate, Harry Markowitz, October 7, 2008:

"In choosing a portfolio, investors should seek broad diversification. Further, they should understand that equities—and corporate bonds also—involve risk; that markets inevitably fluctuate; and their portfolio should be such that they are willing to ride out the bad as well as the good times."

CHAPTER 21

Bond King Blunder

In the office one day, we were chatting about wealth management and amusing ourselves by observing the miscalculations of the financial pundits.

How many of you remember when the "Bond King" Bill Gross pronounced that U.S. bonds should be avoided? Well, Bill soon had a generous serving of egg on his face!

The following brief missive is largely courtesy of Jay Franklin—a thoughtful observer of the financial markets.

Once again, Mr. Market has shown us that he does not play favorites, and nobody is above a serving of humble pie at his table.

One of his victims is none other than the "Bond King" Bill Gross.

You may recall that in early 2011, as part of his "new normal" prediction of extended low economic growth and de-leveraging by consumers, Gross eliminated all his exposure to U.S. government holdings in the Pico Total Return Fund.

With a whopping $243 billion in the fund, this was not easily accomplished. Rather than dumping billions of bonds on the open market, Gross took on derivative positions (such as futures and swaps) to hedge away his interest rate and U.S. dollar risk on U.S. government bonds.

It would be interesting to know who was on the other side of those bets. It could only be large institutional players.

As of August 29, 2011, the bet had not worked out too well for Pimco's Total Return shareholders. The fund returned 3.29% compared to 4.55% for Barclay's Aggregate Bond Index. It was ranked 501st out of 589 bond funds in its category (intermediate-term bond).

To his credit, Gross, with 20/20 hindsight, owned up to his error by saying, "It was a mistake to bet so heavily against the price of U.S. government debt"(Financial Times).

This probably did little to assuage those investors who had added $21.2 billion in new cash to Pimco's Total Return Fund during 2010 and up to July 30, 2011 (estimated net flow from Morningstar Direct).

What are the lessons for investors?

- Relying on economic forecasts as the basis of port-folio decisions can lead to heartbreak.

- Even the most celebrated of pundits can be wrong, and more than once.

Recall that on February 26, 2009, Gross declared the death of equities. Since that time, even with the downturn, the S&P 500 was up 61%.

It is noteworthy that Gross's "guru grade" from CXO Advisory is a below-average 46% (as of May 2009).

Recent investors in the Pimco Total Return Fund should chalk up their underperformance to the tuition that the market never fails to extract from people who believe that some genius will deliver them high returns without high risk.

Hopefully, investors will learn that rather than trying to outsmart the market or beat it to a pulp, they should let the market work for them by owning a risk-appropriate portfolio of index funds, and pay no attention to the gurus.

To quote one of our favorite economists, Paul Samuelson,

"I tell people [that investing] should be dull. It shouldn't be exciting. Investing should be more like watching paint dry or watching grass grow. If you want excitement, take $800 and go to Las Vegas."

CHAPTER 22

STAY IN YOUR SEAT

The day after the sixth game in the World Series one year, a buddy wandered in—remorseful that he, while watching the Cards vs. Rangers, had gotten up out of his seat to go out in his backyard with his dogs (to do who knows what) only to return to his seat and discover that he had missed the walk-off home run by Freeze—arguably the climactic play of the season!

Fortunately, he did have his DVR and was able to replay the excitement he missed while out of his seat.

We view investing similarly. You need to stay in your seat and not vacillate back and forth in and out of the market. You might miss the excitement, and no replay options exist.

Sure, sometimes the excitement is stressful, but who can dismiss the big-picture trend?

Dow Jones Industrial Average (1900 - Present Monthly)

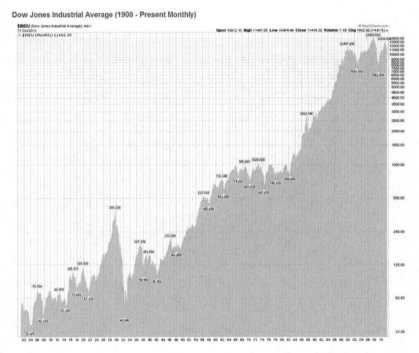

Market timing is alluring, but the requirement for success is to be right twice—when to get out and when to get back in—over and over. We have never found evidence of anyone successfully practicing this tactic over a statistically significant period of time.

Market timers get out hoping they have called a market top or get in hoping they have called a market bottom. But then the agonizing work begins, because market timers not only have to be right on when to get out of their seat but also when to get back in their seat. It is this second decision that is so terribly difficult. When markets move up or down, they do so very quickly.

History demonstrates that if investors miss the best market days their long-term returns are dramatically reduced.

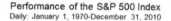

Performance of the S&P 500 Index
Daily: January 1, 1970-December 31, 2010

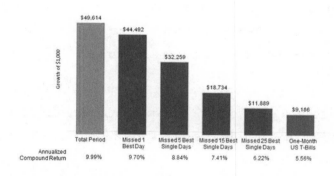

	Total Period	Missed 1 Best Day	Missed 5 Best Single Days	Missed 15 Best Single Days	Missed 25 Best Single Days	One-Month US T-Bills
Growth of $1,000	$49,614	$44,492	$32,259	$18,734	$11,889	$9,186
Annualized Compound Return	9.99%	9.70%	8.84%	7.41%	6.22%	5.56%

Performance data for January 1970-August 2008 provided by CRSP; performance data for September 2008-December 2009 provided by Bloomberg. The S&P data are provided by Standard & Poor's Index Services Group. US bonds and bills data © Stocks, Bonds, Bills, and Inflation Yearbook™, Ibbotson Associates, Chicago (annually updated work by Roger G. Ibbotson and Rex A. Sinquefield).
Indexes are not available for direct investment. Their performance does not reflect the expenses associated with the management of an actual portfolio. Dimensional Fund Advisors is an investment advisor registered with the Securities and Exchange Commission. Information contained herein is compiled from sources believed to be reliable and current, but accuracy should be placed in the context of underlying assumptions. This publication is distributed for educational purposes and should not be considered investment advice or an offer of any security for sale. Past performance is not a guarantee of future results. Unauthorized copying, reproducing, duplicating, or transmitting of this material is prohibited.

Actually—and we don't share this with everyone—we think we may have found the ultimate market predictor: Chinese fortune sticks!

What the heck, everything else has been tried. Hemline indicators, Republican or Democratic victories, seasonal market timing, Ouija boards, market technical indicators, and other fruitless ideas, ad nauseam.

We don't believe we can time the markets. We don't believe anybody can do it more than once in a row.

The chart on the following page, courtesy of Index Fund Advisors, demonstrates the abject failure of 32 market timing newsletters over the decade from January 1988 through December 1997.

We do believe that the emotional stress of watching the value of investments decline—over even a short period of time—is more than the majority of investors can bear.

Here's our free advice: The next time the financial press or the talking heads or your friends start preaching doom-and-gloom or happy-days, please set back in your chair, take a deep breath, and ask yourself:

1. Do I have a plan?

2. Do I have a well-reasoned asset allocation strategy?

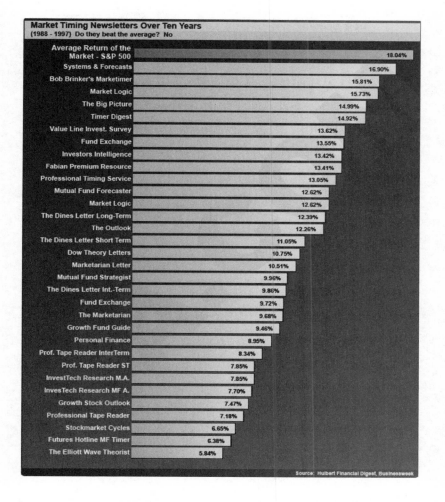

3. Do I have a well-reasoned set of investment vehicles?

4. Do I have enough time to weather inter-period market drawdowns?

If you answer "yes" to all four questions, just do nothing!

If you answer "no" to any of the questions, find a great financial advisor. They are out there!

Here's a thought from Zvi Bodie, professor of finance, Boston University School of Management, Ph.D. MIT., from the fifth edition of his classic tome *Investments*:

> "*Statistical research has shown that . . . stock prices seem to follow a random walk with no discernible predictable patterns that investors can exploit. Such findings are now taken to be evidence of market efficiency, that is, evidence that market prices reflect all currently available information . Only new information will move stock prices, and this information is equally likely to be good or bad news.*"

Please, remain seated.

CHAPTER 23

SOVEREIGN DEBT RATINGS

In August 2011, Standard & Poor's downgraded U.S. government debt from a top-rated AAA to AA+. [1]Standard & Poor's also threatened to downgrade the debt of many European nations.

In the weeks preceding the downgrade of the U.S. government debt event, some market observers expected a downgrade to result in higher interest rates and lower stock returns. It then appeared that those same market observers expected the downgrade of the European nations to result in higher interest rates and lower stock returns for those European nations.

Well, what really happened after the downgrade of U.S. government debt?

After the downgrade, yields on U.S. government securities fell across the term spectrum as investors around the world fled to the safe haven of U.S. bonds.

U.S. stocks experienced negative returns in the following weeks but logged positive performance from the day of the downgrade to the month end.[2]

What would happen if many European nations are downgraded?

That's the $64,000 question, because neither we nor anybody else really knows. We will provide historical data for your consideration.

Debt downgrade events raise questions about whether changes in sovereign debt ratings impact the financial markets.

The short answer is that results are mixed, and that many other factors affect a country's cost of capital and stock market returns.

Regarding bond markets, history offers examples of major developed countries that experienced a credit downgrade without a significant rise in interest rates.[3] Examples include Australia, Canada, and Japan which lost their top ratings in 1986, 1992, and 1998, respectively.

Other research suggests that countries with high credit ratings may withstand a downgrade better than countries with lower ratings. One study looked at sovereign credit rating downgrades since 1990 and found that bond yields changed little among countries downgraded from the highest Triple-A rating. However, countries with lower credit ratings (single-A or below) experienced significant interest rate increases following their downgrade.[4]

Another question is whether the U.S. downgrade has played a role in the U.S. stock market downturn. Research does not provide convincing evidence.

The chart in this chapter summarizes stock market performance of respectively upgraded and downgraded countries before and after a ratings change. This chart is based on a study of ratings changes made by Moody's from 1983 to 2009. During the 27-year period, the ratings agency made 71 upgrades and 25 downgrades to governments in the developed (EAFE) and emerging markets tracked by Morgan Stanley Capital Index (MSCI).

The study identified the date of each change and logged each country's market performance in the 12 months before and 12 months after the event. Each country's market returns were compared to the respective market index and the excess return averaged for all events. (Excess return refers to performance above or below the respective market index, either MSCI EAFE or MSCI Emerging Markets, as appropriate.)

On the following page is a chart demonstrating equity market performance before and after Moody's rating changes from 1983-2009.

The analysis in the following chart was conducted by Dimensional Fund Advisors using sovereign bond rating data from Moody's Investors Services, "Sovereign Default and Recovery Rates, 1983–2009." Returns are in U.S dollars and represent performance in excess of MSCI EAFE Index for developed markets and MSCI Emerging Markets Index for emerging markets. A positive excess return indicates market outperformance; a negative excess return indicates underperformance.

	Cumulative Return in Excess of Market	
	12 Months Before Rating Change	12 Months After Rating Change
Sovereign Bond Upgrade	13.83%	3.87%
Sovereign Bond Downgrade	−6.56%	3.73%

The table reports the return of an equal-weighted, event-time portfolio. Past performance is no guarantee of future results.

The aggregate results show that:

- Stock markets of upgraded countries out-performed their respective market index in the twelve months before the rating change (13.83%).

- Stock markets in downgraded countries aggregately under-performed the market index before the event.

However—and this is important:

Cumulative returns in the 12 months following a ratings change were almost the same for the upgraded and downgraded countries (3.87% vs. 3.73%).5

These results suggest that market prices reflect all available information and expectations about a country's economic prospects—including the possibility of a ratings change.

These results further suggest that if an investor can predict news in advance, then that investor might have an edge on other investors.

By the time a country's debt rating is upgraded or downgraded, the market has already integrated the news into prices. Stock markets reflected positive economic developments prior to a ratings upgrade and negative developments before a ratings downgrade. After the event, markets did not appear to perform much differently, in aggregate.

Conclusion: This research underscores the importance of looking to market prices for signals about the fiscal health and prospects of a country or a company. Based on the foregoing analysis, markets appear to work faster and more accurately than ratings firms to assess a country's financial condition and evaluate the potential impact on its cost of capital and equity market. Therefore, we encourage our clients to turn a deaf ear to the noise that the financial pundits make their living proffering.

Rather than worrying about what the markets might do—heck, we all know they are going to fluctuate—let's spend our time figuring out how we should invest with our uniquely personal goals, values, needs, resources, and obligations driving our decisions.

We'll close with a quote from legendary value investor, Benjamin Graham:

> *"Most of the time common stocks are subject to irrational*
> *and excessive price fluctuations in both directions as the*
> *consequence of the ingrained tendency of most people*
> *to speculate or gamble . . .to give way to hope,*
> *fear and greed."*

ENDNOTES AND REFERENCES:

A sovereign credit rating is an assessment of a government's ability to pay its debts.

[1]The U.S. had held S&P's top rating since 1941. S&P made the announcement after business hours on Friday, August 5, 2011, but word of the downgrade leaked during the day. Although timing of the announcement was a surprise, the downgrade was mostly expected, as S&P had issued a negative long-term outlook for the U.S. in April and July. The other top credit agencies, Moody's Investors Service and Fitch Ratings, maintained top ratings for the U.S.

Two weeks following the downgrade, the U.S. market, as measured by the Russell 3000 Index, logged a negative 6.82% return (August 5–19). However, from the day of the announcement to month end, the market returned a positive 1.6%. (Russell data,©Russell Investment Group 1995–2011.)

[2]Tom Lauricella, "Lessons of Lower Ratings," *Wall Street Journal*, July 30, 2011.

[3]Ivan Rudolph-Shabinsky and Dennis Shen, "When 'Risk-Free' Isn't Risk Free: The Impact of a U.S. Treasury Downgrade" (white paper, Alliance Bernstein, June 30, 2011).

[4]The 12-month aggregate excess performance prior to the ratings change was statistically significant, while the 12-month returns after the ratings change were not.

Warburton Capital wishes to thank and acknowledge Bryan Harris, senior editor with Dimensional Fund Advisors, for his contributions to this data. Past performance is no guarantee of future results.

CHAPTER 24

FINANCIAL WELLNESS

Once we had the privilege of speaking about financial wellness to the associates of a Senior Living firm. As most employers know, employee wellness is good for everybody. Healthy employees have better attendance and better morale. Feeling unqualified to discuss physical wellness, we developed a presentation on financial wellness, the outline of which covered three points:

- Defining financial wellness

- Achieving financial wellness

- Maintaining financial wellness

DEFINING FINANCIAL WELLNESS

Our view for a working definition for financial wellness has been forged as a result of discussions with hundreds of folks.

We start our discussions with this question: What is important to you about money?

This leads to a variety of responses. Frankly, there appears to be a strong correlation between age (or maturity or wisdom or whatever) and the answers our question solicits.

Youngsters often say things like:

- I like money so I can buy stuff!

Older folks often say things like:

- I don't want to outlive my money

- I want to take care of my family

- I like to give it away

- Money gives me freedom

- Money lets me live the way I want to live

- Money represents security, however illusory

So—when it comes to defining financial wellness, permit us to synthesize the responses of folks as the following:

> *Financial wellness exists when a family or person*
> *can live worry free the way they want to live*
> *for as long as they live.*

Let's think about that for a minute. We live for an indeterminable period of time, so throughout that life period—be it 5 more years or 50 more years—financial wellness implies a reality where:

- At some point in your life, work is optional.

- You are free from financial worries.

- Living the way you want to live is practical.

- You won't outlive your money.

Fantastic. Work is optional! No financial worries! Your lifestyle is sustainable! It doesn't matter how long you live!

So, how do we achieve financial wellness?

ACHIEVING FINANCIAL WELLNESS

This exercise sends us on an initial quest to figure out how much money we need and how to accumulate that amount.

Maybe you've seen the advertisement on TV where the guy is trying to figure out his number. The neighbor has a number under his arm, and the comic figure of the commercial thinks his number is a "gazillion."

Well—we think we've figured out what the number is for most folks. As a general guideline:

Multiply your net monthly need by 300.

If you are 65, the above will be close. (Of course, individual age, health, facts, and circumstances vary).

Having derived your number, there are a number of paths one can go down to amass that amount. Some paths are quick and easy, while some are slow and tedious.

Quick and easy:

- Inheritance

- Win the lottery

Slow and tedious:

- Build a business and sell it for a handsome amount

- Work for an employer with a generous retirement account

- Possess assets today which grow—unmolested— over a long period of time

- Save systematically and let those assets grow—unmolested

It really doesn't matter how you get there—you just want to get there!

Which of the above seems most likely to work for you?

This is a point we would be pleased to concern ourselves with toward assessing realistic probabilities and plans for financial wellness thereafter.

Maintaining Financial Wellness

We view the primary component of maintaining financial wellness to be maintaining access to currency. Think about this a bit. Wealth is really irrelevant if you don't have currency.

Think about all of the companies that were asset rich and cash poor and ended up on the shores of bankruptcy. Lack of currency sunk the ship.

Imagine that you owned $100,000,000 worth of land in the Brazilian rain forest, but there were no buyers. Lack of currency is a huge impediment when it comes to paying the bills.

The above examples are real and far-fetched, yet, we offer them to illustrate the point that maintaining financial wellness starts with maintaining access to currency for an extended period of time while simultaneously maintaining an inventory of other assets that can be systematically liquidated at terms that achieve the investors' goals and well before currency assets are exhausted.

We encourage our clients to spend a purposeful amount of time in pursuit of fulfilling their personal goals. An observation from the Irish...yes, we think of you Paddy O—writer, poet and philosopher, Oscar Wilde:

"No man is rich enough to buy back his past."

CHAPTER 25

WORRY FUEL

In August 2011 when the global equity markets were in a tail-spin, we received numerous phone calls from buddies who believed it would be a great time to buy stocks.

Although we never engage in market-timing exercises, I do want to congratulate my buddies for having the courage to buy when the rest of the world wanted to sell.

The surge in stock prices around the world over the past six months (not to mention Q1-2012) serves as a reminder that the markets have a mind of their own.

Six months before, the outlook for stock prices appeared to be fading from grim to grimmer.

Congressional leaders were wrangling unsuccessfully to craft a deficit reduction plan; Standard & Poor's had removed its AAA rating on U.S. Treasury obligations; and Greece appeared one step away from defaulting on its debt.

Yet, just when many investors least expected it, stocks staged a powerful rally.

From the low of last year on October 3 through March 30:

- The S&P 500 Index rebounded 28.1%.

- The Russell 2000 Index jumped 36.2%.

The occasionally accurate adage, "Bull markets climb a wall of worry," was certainly supported.

Let's look at a chronology of the dreadful news that the markets have ridden to gains over the past eight months:

Caution: We may have gotten a little overzealous with the following 25 examples of dreadful and/or confusing news.

August 5, 2011:

- S&P downgrades U.S. Treasury debt to AA+ from AAA; stocks plunge in the biggest selloff since 2008.

September 3, 2011:

- Journalist: "The U.S. economy slammed into a wall in August, failing to add new jobs for the first time in nearly a year."

September 5, 2011:

- Gold reaches a record high of $1,895 per oz. (London Fix).

September 19, 2011:

- Wall Street chief equity strategist: "I don't think we've seen the lows for the year by any stretch. Things have to get much worse before they get better."

September 23, 2011:

- Journalist: "The world economy once again stands on a precipice."

September 26, 2011:

- Investor: "I don't see anything changing in the next two or three years."

October 1, 2011:

- Economist cover story: "Unless politicians act more boldly, the world economy will keep heading towards a black hole."

October 3, 2011:

- U.S. stock prices slump to their lows of the year: 1,099.23 for the S&P 500 and 609.49 for the Russell 2000 Index.

October 13, 2011:

- Census Bureau reports the weakest income growth over a ten-year period since records began in 1967.

October 20, 2011:

- Col. Muammar el-Qaddafi killed by Libyan rebel forces.

November 20, 2011:

- Consumer goods CEO: "Consumers everywhere continue to be cautious and hesitant to spend."

November 21, 2011:

- U.S. Congressional "super committee" fails to reach deficit reduction agreement.

November 24, 2011:

- Market strategist: "Earnings growth is very quickly decelerating."

November 28, 2011:

- Moody's Investors Service warns that multiple countries could default on their debt.

November 29, 2011:

- AMR Corp., parent of American Airlines, files for bankruptcy.

December 10, 2011:

- Detroit's mayor predicts the city will run out of cash by April 2012.

January 6, 2012:

- Gasoline prices are at the highest point ever for a new year.

January 18, 2012:

- World Bank: "Developed and developing-country growth rates could fall by as much or more than in 2008–09."

January 18, 2012:

- Eastman Kodak files for bankruptcy.

January 25, 2012:

- Report from Davos World Economic Forum: "Global elite fears renewed downturn."

February 13, 2012:

- Journalist: "There is still plenty that could go wrong in Europe, while U.S. economic growth remains slow and corporate earnings are looking less and less robust."

February 27, 2012:

- Money manager: "This is a business-as-usual over-priced market and you'll get a zero return for seven years."

March 2, 2012:

- Eurostat reports that Eurozone unemployment in January reached 10.7%, the highest in fifteen years.

March 12, 2012:

- Strategist: "The stock market has effectively doubled since the March 2009 low, and we're still in redemption territory for equity funds."

March 19, 2012:

- Journalist: "Expectations for earnings have been steadily scaled back this year, as the mood among companies has worsened."

Summary

The foregoing is an exhausting litany of things to worry about. Yet would worrying about them—or, worse yet—making decisions based on these headlines—have been accretive to investors in any manner? Not recently!

Predictions based on headlines—or even economic forecasts—appear to be as worthless as the sun behind the clouds on a cold day. The next time I feel like I can predict the future, I hope somebody will just take me out to the woodshed like Dear Old Dad never did.

We will close with two missives from legendary British economist, John Maynard Keynes—the father of Keynesian economics—whose ideas have profoundly affected the theories of modern macroeconomics as well as the economic policies of governments.

As he might assist us in the quest for enlightenment:

"A study of the history of opinion is a necessary preliminary to the emancipation of the mind."

As he might inspire us with the spirit of optimism:

"It would not be foolish to contemplate the possibility of a far greater progress still."

REFERENCES:

1. E.S. Browning, "Downgrade Ignites a Global Selloff," *Wall Street Journal*, August 9, 2011.

2. Sudeep Reddy, "Job Growth Grinds to a Halt," *Wall Street Journal*, September 3, 2011.

3. Quotation from Adam Parker, chief U.S. equity strategist Morgan Stanley. Jonathan Cheng, "Wall Street's Optimism Fades," *Wall Street Journal*, September 19, 2011.

4. Chris Giles, "Financial Institutions Stare into the Abyss," *Financial Times*, September 22, 2011.

5. Tom Lauricella, "Pivot Point: Investors Lose Faith in Stocks," *Wall Street Journal*, September 26, 2011.

6. "Be Afraid," *Economist*, October 1, 2011.

7. Phil Izzo, "Bleak News for Americans' Income," *Wall Street Journal*, October 13, 2011.

8. Kareem Fahim, "Qaddafi, Seized by Foes, Meets a Violent End," *New York Times*, October 21, 2011.

9. Quotation from Jim Skinner, chief executive of McDonald's. Jeff Sommer, "From the Mouths of Executives, Little Comfort," *New York Times*, November 20, 2011.

10. Jonathan Cheng and Brendan Conway, "Panel's Failure Sinks Stocks," *Wall Street Journal*, November 21, 2011.

11. Quotation from David Rosenberg, chief market strategist, Gluskin, Sheff & Associates. Tom Petruno, "Wall Street Gets Cautious on Earnings," *Los Angeles Times*, November 24, 2011.

12. Brendan Conway and Steven Russolillo, "No Year-End Stock Surge in Sight," *Wall Street Journal*, November 26, 2011.

13. Liz Alderman and Stephen Castle, "Dire Warnings Are Building on European Debt Crisis," *New York Times*, November 29, 2011.

14. "Nowhere to Run—The Motor City Flirts with Fiscal Disaster," *Economist*, December 10, 2011.

15. Ronald D. White, "Gas Prices Ring in 2012 at a High," *Los Angeles Times*, January 6, 2012.

16. Chris Giles, "World Bank Warns on the Risk of Global Economic Meltdown," *Financial Times*, January 18, 2012.

17. Chris Giles, "Pessimism Hangs in Mountain Air," *Financial Times*, January 25, 2012.

18. Tom Lauricella and Jonathan Cheng, "Too Late to Jump Aboard?" *Wall Street Journal*, February 13, 2012.

19. Ajay Makan, "S&P 500 at Post-Crisis Peak but Investors Remain Wary," *Financial Times*, February 25, 2012.

20. Quotation from Jeremy Grantham, chief investment strategist, GMO. Leslie P. Norton, "Not So fast: Coping with Slow Growth," *Barron's*, February 27, 2012.

21. Brian Blackstone, "Poor Economic Data Slam Europe," *Wall Street Journal*, March 2, 2012.

22. Quotation from Liz Ann Sonders, chief investment strategist, Charles Schwab, Nikolaj Gammeltoft, Inyoun Hwang, and Whitney Kisling, "The Bull Turns Three. Where's the Party?"*Business Week*, March 12, 2012.

23. Ajay Makan, "Wall Street Braces For Hit to Soaring Markets," *Financial Times*, March 19, 2012.

We wish to thank Weston Wellington, vice president, Dimensional Fund Advisors, for his objective perspective, contributions to this chapter and the extensive data.

CHAPTER 26

FIVE FACTORS

A client came to me with a glazed look in his eyes. He had just left an exciting sales presentation by the prominent investment firm—Dewey, Cheatum, & Howe (DCH) (not their real name). DCH had revealed their best idea right now for beating the market.(Somebody in the firm had created a new product, and it fell to the client-facing advisors to sell this product to any client for whom it was suitable.)

Their best idea right now turned out to be a clever structured product.

I remembered that I had done an analysis of a similar product several years ago, which revealed a less than ideal outcome that I reviewed with my client.

Believing it would be a good time for an information exchange, I travelled a more useful road. I retrieved a one page hand-out that revealed how to beat the market—with a reasonable degree of certainty—in a completely different way.

Five Factors Help Determine Expected Return
Annual Average Returns
1927–2011

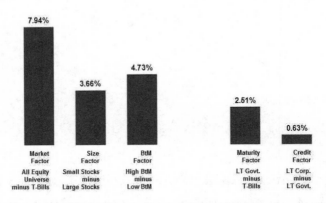

Equity factors provided by Fama/French. Maturity factor and credit factor data (1927–1972) provided by © Stocks, Bonds, Bills, and Inflation Yearbook©, Ibbotson Associates, Chicago (annually updated work by Roger G. Ibbotson and Rex A. Sinquefield). Credit factor data (1973–present) provided by Barclays Bank PLC. Indices are not available for direct investment. Their performance does not reflect the expenses associated with the management of an actual portfolio.

The five risk dimensions that academic research has identified to determine expected return are shown here. The five factors(working from left to right in the picture) are:

1. Market Factor

2. Size Factor

3. BtM Factor

4. Maturity Factor

5. Credit Factor

Market Factor—Stocks versus Bonds

Stocks have higher expected returns than bonds. From 1927 through 2011, the all equity (stocks) universe delivered an annual average return that was 7.94% greater than T-bills.

Size Factor—Small Cap Stocks versus Large Cap Stocks

Small cap stocks have higher expected returns than large cap stocks. From 1927 through 2011, small cap stocks delivered an annual average return that was 3.66% greater than large cap stocks.

Book-To-Market (BtM)—Value Stocks versus Growth Stocks

Stocks with high book-to-market quotients (value stocks) have higher expected returns than stocks with low book-to-market quotients (growth stocks). From 1927 through 2011, value stocks delivered an annual average return that was 4.73% greater than growth stocks.

Maturity Factor—Long-Term Governments versus T-Bills

Long-term government bonds have a higher expected return than T-bills. From 1927 through 2011, long-term government bonds delivered an annual average return that was 2.51% greater than T-bills.

Credit Factor—Long-Term Corporate versus Long-Term Government

Long-term corporate bonds have a higher expected return than long-term government bonds. From 1927 through 2011, long-term corporate bonds delivered an annual average return that was 0.63% greater than long-term government bonds.

Of course, a further study is imperative to grasp that the compensation for return increment delivered by the risk factors was delivered with higher risk—volatility!

There Ain't No Free Lunch!

CHAPTER 27

ARE INVESTORS LOOKING FOR A GURU?

A client sent us an article from the *New York Times*. It's great to be in this industry and share information with our friends and clients toward the goal of mutually knowing more.

The article, by Certified Financial Planner Carl Richards, conveyed pearls of wisdom that are, I believe, obvious, part of the collective wisdom, yet difficult for investors to internalize. ("Your Misguided Search for a Money Guru,"*New York Times 2012.*Carl Richards is a certified financial planner in Park City, Utah. His book, *The Behavior Gap*, was published earlier in 2012.)

Executive Summary: Investors are looking for a money guru to do the impossible, which is to predict the market. Richards goes on to summarize the important things that make a difference: the things we can control like systematic

saving, asset allocation, fees, and utilization of our most valuable resource—time.

In our view, investors would be better off if, instead of
looking for a money guru, they looked for an advisor who
would take the time to fully understand their goals, values,
needs, resources, and obligations, and thereafter, formulate a
uniquely personal plan to achieve those goals.

A lot of people ask me where I think the stock market is
headed. It's a common question, but it does get more frequent
when the Dow is in the news for crossing some barrier, like
reaching 13,000.

Why do we look for someone to divine the future for us?

I think we all know that predicting where the market will
head is next to impossible. It's even more unlikely that we'll
find a guru who will predict it correctly again and again. Yet
we still look.

Maybe we've always been this way. We look for someone,
anyone, who can take the complex and seemingly random
landscape we're trying to navigate and make sense of it.

We do this in many areas of life, seeking shortcuts or
mental tricks we can use to find an answer. Think about the
weather. The forces that control it can be complex, and despite
rather predictable seasonal changes, it can feel random on any

given day. So even though the weather forecast is often wrong, we keep checking.

When it comes to money, we look for a guru to answer questions like:

- With the Dow back at 13,000, is now a good time to invest?

- With the Dow back at 13,000, is now a good time to sell?

- What will happen in Europe?

- Should I invest in real estate?

- When are certificate of deposit rates going to improve?

I'm reminded of a meeting I had with an investment committee of a sizable endowment fund.

The members bemoaned the fact that all they really wanted was for someone to tell them when the market was going down or up so they could know when to get out and when to get in. They said it was fine if it wasn't a perfect system, but surely the "pros" could get close.

Unfortunately, they can't. No one rings a bell when things are about to turn around. Think back to March 2009. Who was predicting a market run like we've seen since then?

I've also had multiple people tell me that while you can't time the market (how silly!), you can "just tell" when it's getting close to the top. You can just "feel it." But I don't recall that working out very well either.

It's easy to find people willing to tell you where they think things are going. Jim Cramer will tell you where he thinks 40 stocks a day are headed. Alan Greenspan was more than willing to tell us that a "national severe price distortion seems most unlikely in the United States."

I don't fault people for being wrong, but I do think we should stop listening unless we're doing it for fun. You know, like going to the circus.

Another challenge when searching for gurus is that they often seem to be saying different things. What are we supposed to do when we read these two quotes within days of the other?

"We've been counseling investors that it's time to get back in the market." —Douglas Cote, chief market strategist at ING Investment Management.

"We think the next pullback could be particularly sharp." *"There is very little chart support beneath the market, in our view, so when a drop comes, get your fingers out of the way."* S&P Capital IQ.

So what if we finally stopped looking? Imagine what life would be like if we built a plan that didn't depend on a guru and instead spent time focused on what we do have some control over, like how much we save, our asset allocation, and how much we pay in fees.

What if instead of searching for the guru, we read a book or went to a movie? Looking for something that you will never find is no way to spend our most valuable resource: time.

CHAPTER 28

DESIGNING A PLAN FOR WEALTH ACCUMULATION

A client once told us he'd had a liquidity event! Terrific! (This seems to be occurring frequently as our clients pass the baton of their enterprises to the next generation.)

This was a married gentleman whose primary goals for his money were to "not outlive it" and "not have to start over." There was no evidence of a "money is a scorecard" mentality, so we felt mathematically tasked to figure out how much currency escrow (short-term investment grade global bonds or STIGGB) would this client need to achieve his two primary goals.

Working backwards, we determined the lifestyle burn rate and sources of dependable mailbox income. It developed that this client would continue to accumulate wealth given the surplus of mailbox income to lifestyle burn rate, if the mailbox income continued.

So, how much risk did we take with the cash from the liquidity event in capital market securities given that:

- The client would continue to wealth accumulate,

- The cash from this liquidity event was sufficient to achieve the primary goals, and

- There was significant equity in unsold enterprise assets

The answer was "not very much"! This was an example of an investor who needs to have asset preservation put far ahead of asset appreciation.

So, our recommendations were:

- Migrate a purposeful amount of cash into STIGGB with the simple goal of out-earning cash and out-earning inflation.

- Migrate the remainder cash into an endowment model (60% stocks and 40% bonds) over the following 36 months. Manage this sub-portfolio against a conservative pro-forma.

- Take gains when the sub-portfolio is ahead of the conservative pro-forma.

- Utilize sale proceeds to increase the currency escrow until "wealthy to 100" is significantly overfunded.

Of course, there were other considerations, not the least of which were monitoring cash accumulation against a goal, investing surplus cash systematically, or distributing cash from the currency escrow if need be.

Is this conservative? Yes. We recommended this conservative path because our client has enough and it speaks to what our client values about money.

We enjoy helping folks make work optional and maintain that status. It's always a great intellectual challenge involving both emotional and practical issues. Helping folks with financial goals always involves a thorough understanding of what we believe to be the four most important questions each investor must be able to answer:

1. What rate of return risk do you need to take with your investments to enjoy the standard of living throughout retirement that you enjoy today and not outlive your money?

2. How long will you have to work before you can afford to retire?

3. How much can you afford to spend in retirement and not run out of money?

4. How much do you need to be saving on a monthly (or annual) basis to reach your

necessary liquid net worth amount and have your money last to life expectancy?

These questions are just the tip of the iceberg, but, they provide enough data to begin deriving a plan that is realistic and will serve its intended purpose—Make Work Optional.

As regards the recent success of our buddy, which was obtained after several decades of hard work and risk taking, we'll close with a tongue-in-cheek comment from the now deceased Boston Red Sox pitcher, Earl Wilson:

"Success is simply a matter of luck. Just ask any failure!"

Following are a number of questions that need to be answered before any thoughtful planning can be undertaken:

Designing a Plan For Wealth Accumulation

- How much will your desired retirement lifestyle cost?

- How many years will you be retired?

- How much money do you need to accumulate to be reasonably confident you won't outlive your money?

- How much money do you have today?

- Do you need more money?

  o If "no": Are you going to keep working?

- o If "yes": How much more do you need?

- How much can you save?

- How long can you sustain saving at that level?

- How long will it take to accumulate your required wealth?

- What rate of return risk do you need to take in order to accumulate sufficient wealth?

- What rate of return risk do you need to take in retirement?

"Deriving a realistic plan and executing that plan
increase the odds of making work optional
and maintaining that status."—Tom Warburton

CHAPTER 29

CERTAINTY AND THE LONG-TERM INVESTOR

A frequent comment from hesitant investors is that uncertainty is what keeps them out of the financial markets. "I'll stay in cash until the direction becomes clearer," they say. One might pose another question: "When has there ever been total clarity?"

Alternatively, people who are already in the market after a strong rally, as we have seen in recent years, nervously eye media commentary about possible pullbacks and say, "Maybe now is a good time to move to the sidelines."

While seemingly informed decisions to buy or sell stocks are understandable, they are also unnecessary. Strategic rebalancing provides a solution, which we will explore in a moment.

But first, think back to March 2009. With equity markets having suffered a severe 16-month decline, the Associated Press provided its readers with five signs the stock market had bottomed out and followed that up with five signs that it hadn't. Fabulous equivocating if we ever saw it!

The case for a turn was convincing. Trading volume was up, the slide in the U.S. economy appeared to be slowing, banks were returning to profitability, commodity prices had bounced, and many retail investors had capitulated and gone to cash.

However, there also was a case for more pain. Toxic assets still weighed on banks' balance sheets, economic signals were patchy, short-covering was driving rallies, the Madoff scandal had shaken confidence, and fear was widespread.

Hindsight affirms that March 2009 marked the bottom of that bear market. In the intervening period of five-plus years, major equity indices have rebounded to all-time or multi-year highs.

Exhibit 1 on the following page shows the cumulative performance of a few major global and domestic indices in the approximately 15 months of the bear market that began in November 2007, and then the cumulative performance in the subsequent recovery period through May 2014.

You can see there have been substantial gains across the board since the market bottom.

Moreover, while annualized performance over the six-and-a-half years from November 2007 is not impressive, there has been a lot less pain for those who did not bail out in March 2009. Those who got out of the market at the very bottom and waited for certainty probably realized substantial losses and certainly (that word again) did not benefit from the recovery.

However, in keeping with our exploration of certainty, let us keep in mind that these past five years of recovery in equity markets have also been marked by periods of major uncertainty.

Exhibit 1 MARKET PERFORMANCE: FINANCIAL CRISIS AND POST-CRISIS
Returns (USD %)

	11/2007– 02/2009	03/2009– 05/2014	11/2007– 05/2014	11/2007– 05/2014
	Cumulative	Cumulative	Cumulative	Annualized
MSCI World Value	-54.38%	157.24%	17.34%	2.49%
Russell 2000 Index	-48.34%	213.33%	61.87%	7.69%
MSCI World Small Cap	-52.80%	217.93%	50.07%	6.44%
MSCI World IMI	-52.03%	163.11%	26.22%	3.65%

Past performance is not a guarantee of future results. Indices are not available for direct investment; therefore, their performance does not reflect the expenses associated with the management of an actual portfolio.

In 2011, Europe was gripped by a sovereign debt crisis. On our side of the Atlantic, Washington engaged in periodic brinksmanship over the U.S. debt ceiling. In Asia, China grappled with the transition from an export-led to a domestic-driven economy.

Around any of these events, views varied broadly about likely outcomes and the influence on financial markets. What were we to do with all that conflicting commentary?

The fact exists that professionals struggle to consistently add value by analyzing macroeconomic events. This is evidenced repeatedly in surveys of actively managed funds versus passively managed index returns.

Additionally, history suggests that those looking for certainty before investing could be setting themselves up for a long wait. There is always something to fret about. Recently, the focus has been on low volatility, particularly when compared to 2008–09.

Sage gurus muse over whether risk is being appropriately priced and whether volatility is being unnaturally suppressed by central banks' explicit forward guidance about fiscal policy.

Just as in March 2009, one does not have to look far to find intelligent-sounding arguments in support of why the market has topped out, alongside equally compelling rationale of why the rally might continue for some time.

Again, what are investors supposed to make of all this conflicting conjecture? One way is to debate the market implications of news and to try to anticipate what might happen next. But which view do you embrace? There are cogent-sounding arguments for multiple scenarios.

An alternative approach is much simpler. It begins by accepting the market price as a fair reflection of the collective opinions of millions of market participants. Having drawn this conclusion, rather than betting against the market, you get to work with the market. This implies building a diversified portfolio around the known dimensions of expected returns according to your uniquely individual needs and risk tolerance, not according to the opinions of media and market pundits about what will happen tomorrow, next week, or next month.

This approach involves staying disciplined with a chosen asset allocation and regularly rebalancing your portfolio. Under this approach, a portion of stocks is sold after a market advance or a portion of stocks is purchased after a market decline. The trigger for rebalancing is not media speculation but the discipline of maintaining a percentage weighted asset allocation.

Let's assume you have settled on a portfolio allocation of 60% in stocks and 40% in bonds. Suppose a year goes by and stocks have rallied such that the balance has shifted to 70%/30%. In this case, rebalancing dictates taking some money out of stocks and buying bonds. When stocks decline, you take some money out of bonds and buy stocks. Essentially, you consistently buy low and sell high. An additional benefit of this strategy is that you are behaving based on your needs rather than on what the armies of pundits predict will happen in the market next.

Of course, this doesn't mean you can't take an interest in global events. Global events are interesting. However, a rebalancing discipline will spare you from basing your long-term investment strategy on the illusion that somewhere, at some time, certainty will return.

We won't express certainty that the next 87 years will replicate the past 87 years. However, we advise basing planning decisions on the long-term trends of free-enterprise capitalism as opposed to the plethora of financial media headlines that advocate zigging and zagging in perpetuity.

CHAPTER 30

EPILOGUE

I can think of no better way to end this trip through *Timeless Wealth Management* missives than by telling one more story about a buddy.

He came into my office clearly distracted.

We inquired, "What's on your mind?"

"I'm worried about my wife's health-related special needs," he said. "If something happens to me I want her to be taken care of, and I don't know what to do to make sure that her needs are met."

This was clearly a wonderfully responsible concern of a loving husband for a beloved spouse, and we were honored that our buddy shared this with us.

So, how did we help? We don't practice law; however, we had observed a similar scenario when a client had solved for a similar contingent liability by creating a special needs trust for a loved one.

So, we introduced our client to an estate planning expert. After several collaborations, the concern was provided for via a modified special needs trust funded with conservative assets.

A couple of weeks later we ran into our buddy again, and the only thing on his mind was where to take his family for a vacation.

Fantastic! This sounds like what retirement should be all about—taking family vacations! Not to mention that retirement is, in the words of my buddy, Craig, "when there is no dress code, every night is Friday night, and every day is Saturday."

Our mission at Warburton Capital is timeless. We want to help our clients achieve their wealth management goals in a professional, responsive, personal, and efficient manner.

We view the responsibility of being a "personal CFO" as more than just recommending investments. More broadly, it means being there for our clients when any important life or financial decision requires discussion, collaboration, and a well-informed action plan.

Mark Twain once said, "Wrinkles should merely indicate where smiles have been."If the stress of wealth management is contributing more to your wrinkles than the smiles are, perhaps we, or some other like-minded professional, can help?

Wishing each of you a rich life wherein your personal goals are pursued, indulged, and achieved, I remain:

Yours truly,
Tom Warburton